Contents

Crossing Boundaries

Change and Continuity in the History of Learning Disability

Edited by
Lindsay Brigham, Dorothy Atkinson, Mark Jackson,
Sheena Rolph and Jan Walmsley

British Library Cataloguing in Publication Data

A CIP record for this book is available from the British Library

ISBN 1 902519 21 3

© Copyright 2000 BILD Publications

BILD Publications is the publishing office of the
British Institute of Learning Disabilities
Wolverhampton Road
Kidderminster
Worcestershire
United Kingdom
DY10 3PP
Telephone: 01562 850251
Fax: 01562 851970
e-mail: bild@bild.demon.co.uk

BILD Publications are distributed worldwide by
Plymbridge Distributors Limited
Plymbridge House
Estover Road
Plymouth
United Kingdom
PL6 7PZ
Telephone: 01752 202301
Fax: 01752 202333

Printed by
The Cookley Printers Limited
56 Bridge Road
Cookley
Kidderminster
Worcestershire
United Kingdom DY10 3SB

List of contributors

Simone Aspis is a self-employed disability consultant and has undertaken a range of research projects. She has completed a study of the transition phase for young disabled people with the National Foster Care Association and Brent Association of Disabled People. In addition, Simone has written papers on self-advocacy and has developed a new model for *Disability and Society* and *Community Living*. Simone was People First's Parliamentary and Campaigns Worker, where she was successful in ensuring that disabled people with learning difficulties were included in the direct payments legislation, and had previously worked on the Disability Discrimination Act and Civil Rights (Disabled Person) Bills. Simone Aspis describes herself as a special school survivor and was labelled by the standardised psychological tests as having learning difficulties. Simone is currently involved with the 'Free Our People' Campaign and is supporting disabled children with learning difficulties who want to be free to attend a mainstream school.

Dorothy Atkinson is a senior lecturer in the School of Health and Social Welfare at the Open University. Her background is in social work and includes several years' experience of working with people with learning difficulties. Her current interest is in exploring the use of life history work with people with learning difficulties to enable individuals and groups to tell their stories. Her recent book reflects this interest: *An Auto-Biographical Approach to Learning Disability Research* (Ashgate 1997).

Lindsay Brigham is a Staff Tutor for the School of Health and Social Welfare based in the regional centre for the Open University in the North. Her interest in the social history of learning disability stems from studying for an MA in Women's Studies, where she undertook project work with young women with learning difficulties and wrote a dissertation on the history of women with learning difficulties. She has now had some of this work published.

Mabel Cooper is a member of People First, Croydon. She used to be the chair of People First, Croydon and before that the chair and vice chair of People First, London. Her life story was published in the book *Forgotten Lives* (BILD 1997) and was also made into a film shown on BBC television. Her current work involves speaking at conferences and running workshops on the theme of how life-story work can contribute to the history of learning disability.

Dan Goodley is a lecturer and researcher in the Department of Psychology, Bolton Institute. Dan's current research interests centre around the self-advocacy of people labelled as having learning difficulties. He has just completed a book *Politics of resilience: Self-advocacy in the lives of people with learning difficulties*, which draws upon an ethnography of self-advocacy groups and the life stories of self-advocates. He has recently started a two-year Economic and Social Research Council-funded research project on civil rights, self-advocacy and people with learning difficulties.

Mark Jackson is a Senior Lecturer in the Centre for Medical History at the University of Exeter. He has published numerous articles and books on the history of infanticide and the history of mental deficiency. His latest book, entitled *The Borderland of Imbecility: Medicine, Society, and the Fabrication of the Feeble Mind in Late Victorian and Edwardian England*, is due to be published by Manchester University Press in 2000. Drawing on his previous qualifications in immunology and medicine, he is now engaged in a large research project on the history of allergy and asthma.

Duncan Mitchell is a learning disability nurse and currently Head of the School of Nursing at the University of Salford. He has published a number of articles on the history of learning disability nursing and is currently completing his PhD on the same subject.

Maureen Oswin's background is child education and social research. After fourteen years working at Queen Mary's Hospital, Carshalton, with children who had multiple disabilities, she went to the Thomas Coram Research Unit, London, to research the quality of child care in long-stay hospitals. She has written six books based on her studies of institutions. Due to family illness she gave up professional work in the early 1980s to become a full-time carer. She is now retired.

Patricia Potts is a Senior Lecturer in the School of Education at the Open University. Her work for courses which explore barriers to learning and how they might be overcome has led her to ask questions about the design of buildings which are used as learning environments. Her other interests include education in China and Hong Kong, the oral history of disability and education, and the history of teacher education for women.

Sheena Rolph is completing her doctoral thesis at the School of Health and Social Welfare at the Open University. The subject of her research is the history of community care in Norfolk in the twentieth century. Her background is in art history and education, and she has several years' experience of working in adult education with people with learning difficulties. Her main focus of interest continues to be the history of community care and ways of enabling individuals and groups to contribute to this history through the telling of their life stories.

Tim Stainton is a lecturer at the Centre for Applied Social Studies, University of Wales, Swansea. He worked for many years as a service broker, policy analyst and lobbyist for people with a learning disability in Canada before completing his doctorate at the London School of Economics. He has published a theory of rights and learning disability, *Autonomy and Social Policy* (Avebury 1994), and numerous articles on issues of policy, practice, theory and the history of learning disability. He is currently working on a book charting the relationship between reason and human value and how this has influenced the construction of learning disability.

Mary Stuart has worked with people with learning difficulties since 1981, as a tutor, self-advocacy support worker and researcher. She is currently assistant director at the Centre for Continuing Education at the University of Sussex. She has written on life history methods in Oral History (1993, 1995), and on sexuality and women with learning difficulties (1995). She completed her DPhil in 1998 and is currently finishing a book based on this research with women with learning difficulties who lived in convent homes.

Jan Walmsley is a Senior Lecturer in the School of Health and Social Welfare at the Open University. She has developed a particular interest in constructing the history of learning disability from a variety of oral and written sources. She is co-editor of *Forgotten Lives* (BILD 1997), *Health, Welfare and Oral History* (Routledge 1999) and *Good Times, Bad Times* (BILD 2000).

Acknowledgements

The editors would like to thank:
Christine Finch for her patient work in typing and re-typing the manuscript;

John Harris, for his encouragement and suggestions.

Photographs and Illustrations

Grateful acknowledgement is made to the following sources for permission to reproduce the photographs and illustrations in this book:

Baillière Tindall Publishers
David Barron
Dianne Bennell, Local Studies Library, Chesterfield
Mencap
Lucy O'Leary, Corporate Policy Manager, Northgate and Prudhoe
    NHS Trust
Maureen Oswin
Mrs Pearce
Stuart Watson of the Builder Group
Charlotte Wood, Photographer, Marlborough, Wiltshire

Tables and Figures

Introduction

Mark Jackson

Many years ago, when I was a child, I spent one or two weeks of every summer holiday staying with my aunt and uncle, Jo and John, and their two children, Ian and Danny, both of whom have what are now referred to as learning difficulties. As a young boy, I recognised differences between my cousins and myself. They went to separate schools, they were treated distinctively by people who met them, and in some ways they looked different. At the same time, such differences did not seem important. During my time in their house, I played with Ian and Danny, argued and fought with them, ate with them, watched television with them, and went out with them. Indeed, the similarities between my cousins and myself were, and still are, infinitely more noticeable than the differences.

Those childhood holidays near Oxford were instructive in many ways. In particular, I saw how my aunt and uncle struggled with the local education authority to ensure that their children received an appropriate education, how they wrestled with persistent stigma and prejudice, and how they strove to preserve their own mental and physical health in the face of those challenges. Lessons learned during my childhood vacations have not been forgotten. Not only have they constituted a major influence on my own endeavours as a parent but they have also determined and energised my historical interest in learning disabilities.

I want to make three specific points from these episodes in my childhood. In the first instance, it seems clear that any history of learning disability must make the lives and experiences of people such as Ian and Danny central. Indeed, the experiences of people with learning difficulties constitute a critical starting point for any history. But at the same time, the history of learning disability is not solely about people with learning difficulties. To do justice to the richness and complexity of Ian and Danny's lives, any account of their histories must also include their parents, their friends, and their families. Ian and Danny's histories are inextricably bound up with those of Jo and John. In some small way, since I lived with them and loved them and since they continue to inform my life, their histories are also linked to my own history. From this perspective, the history of learning disability is a shared history.

My second point concerns the purpose of researching and writing the history of learning disability. At one level, research should involve the processes of uncovering, listening to, and learning from the experiences of people with learning difficulties. And yet, if we are to comprehend those experiences fully, we need to cast our historical net wide. The labels that have been used to describe people with learning difficulties, the various medical and educational policies that have been imposed, and the diverse stigmas that have been generated at different times have not been produced by people with learning difficulties themselves. On the contrary, they have been manufactured by a variety of social processes. If we are to understand those processes, then we need also to explore and analyse shifting social and political structures, legislative interventions, medical and educational strategies, the ways in which boundaries have been drawn and reinforced, and the fears and anxieties of societies at different times. Only if we pay attention to these facets of the past can we begin to recognise precisely why certain people were institutionalised, sterilised, stigmatised, and excluded. And it is only through a comprehensive, and historically informed, analysis of the past that we can begin to create a future free from such prejudice and stigma.

My final point concerns the identity of, and the relationships between, the various historians engaged in excavating the past. If professional historians continue to exclude the experiences and knowledge of people with learning difficulties from their accounts then they are perpetuating the boundaries and stigmas that they seek to explain. On the other hand, if people with learning difficulties insist that history belongs solely to them, they are closing the door on much knowledge and insight that could help emancipate them from past and present prejudices. If the history of learning disability is a shared history, then the research and writing of that history must be pursued without boundaries. Academics and practitioners, people with learning difficulties and those without, oral historians and historians focusing on written documents (among many others) can and should contribute both individually and collectively to exposing the history of learning disability in its complexity and entirety.

This book is motivated and informed by two closely related convictions: firstly, that boundaries have been drawn, and continue to be drawn, between 'people with learning difficulties' and the 'rest of the population'; and secondly, that those boundaries can, and should, be crossed. The chapters that constitute the book are revised versions of papers presented at two conferences organised and run by the Social History of Learning Disability Research Group at the Open University.[1] Many of the papers presented on those occasions addressed questions relating either to the manner in which boundaries have been drawn, or to the ways in which they have been crossed, in the past: Why have boundaries been drawn between the 'normal' and the 'pathological'? How have boundaries been created and by whom? What institutional and administrative structures have been created to establish or reinforce boundaries? How have boundaries been crossed, and by whom? What have been the social and political implications of drawing or crossing boundaries in different locations at different times? What have been the emotional impacts of boundaries?

It was clear at both conferences that many of these questions continue to have a strong resonance for people with learning difficulties and academics today. For example, at the heart of discussions at those conferences at the Open University lay the difficult question as to who should be writing the history of learning disability: whose history is it? Is the history of learning disability the province of academic historians or the property of people with learning difficulties them-selves? How do we reconcile the differing approaches and differing conclusions drawn by different constituencies? Much of the debate around such questions demonstrated that boundaries between people with and without learning difficulties, and between different academic disciplines and practices, are still being carefully drawn and vigorously defended. It would seem that if we are to give a voice to everyone interested in the history of learning disability then we need ourselves to cross these contemporary boundaries constructively, and to develop an approach to history that integrates different stories at many different levels.

Crossing Boundaries represents a concerted attempt to facilitate that integration and to cross existing disciplinary and political boundaries by exploring in detail some of the debates and dilemmas that have characterised the history of learning disability in the nineteenth and twentieth centuries. The structure of the book is framed by current preoccupations and inspired in particular by three challenging narratives written by people with learning difficulties. In the first chapter, Simone Aspis argues that the process of researching and writing history has too frequently perpetuated the social and political boundaries that are under analysis, carelessly exploiting the lives of people with learning difficulties for professional purposes. As a result, as Simone points out, people with learning difficulties have been excluded from research, refused access to funding, and often denied the power to write their own histories.

The chapters by David Barron and by Mabel Cooper and Dorothy Atkinson amply demonstrate the drawbacks and dangers of excluding people with learning difficulties, both from society and from writing history. Narrated with considerable force, David's chapter not only provides a compelling account of the ways in which boundaries impact, both physically and emotionally, on people's lives, but also challenges us to expose the multiple political, social, and cultural forces that have created those boundaries. Mabel's chapter continues this theme by highlighting the importance of tempering any documentary history with the experiences of people with learning difficulties. In this innovative and challenging chapter, Mabel and Dorothy compare Mabel's account of her life with the account found in her hospital case notes. In addition to exploring the boundaries that have been drawn and crossed in Mabel's life from a variety of perspectives, the approach used in this chapter suggests ways in which academics and people with learning difficulties can combine their experiences and expertise to produce shared histories.

While acknowledging the primacy of accounts provided by people with learning difficulties themselves, it is also important to recognise that the experiences of Simone, David, and Mabel have been strongly determined by broad social and political contexts. As Mabel and Dorothy point out, Mabel (like David and many others) was admitted to hospital under the terms of the Mental Deficiency Acts of 1913 and 1927. In order to understand the lives of people with learning difficulties in the twentieth century, it is therefore necessary both to explore and expose the ideology, origins, politics, and implementation of such legislation, and to demonstrate the diverse ways in which medical categories and labels have been created.

These questions provide the focus for the next chapters. In Chapter 4, Lindsay Brigham exploits a number of historical sources to explore ways in which the creation of boundaries between people labelled as 'mentally defective' and the rest of the population were linked to middle-class fears that 'mental defectives' were a dangerous source of 'pollution' and contamination within society. As Lindsay suggests, within the context of changing patterns of work and domestic management, such fears were strongly interwoven with late nineteenth-century attitudes to women, by the perceived threat of 'racial degeneration', and by anxieties about the behaviour and morality of the lower classes.

Significantly, these ideological concerns carried practical consequences. In particular, the notion of difference was cemented and consolidated in the form of institutions designed initially to educate, and subsequently to segregate, large numbers of people labelled as 'mental defectives'. By analysing the architectural strategies employed in the past to construct boundaries, to legitimate labels, and to establish control, Patricia Potts demonstrates the manner in which institutional buildings and regimes both reflected and reinforced dominant ideologies. Although many institutions have now closed, and although community care and inclusion now carry greater political weight than segregation, it is important to recognise that the legacy of nineteenth-century asylums and colonies is evident in a number of locations: in the continuation of special schools; in the lives and experiences of people such as David and Mabel; and in Simone's fervent sense of exclusion from historical research.

As Sheena Rolph argues in Chapter 6, the boundaries constructed so forcefully around the turn of the twentieth century were not necessarily impermeable. People did manage to cross institutional, geographical, and personal boundaries. Employing a splendid collection of original archival sources, Sheena charts the life of one woman, Alice Chapman, who successfully negotiated a variety of 'border crossings' before eventually escaping from the oppressive grip of the 1913 Mental Deficiency Act and achieving independence. Although Alice's story is an inspiring narrative of individual energy and persistence, it is crucial to remember that she only achieved her own home at the age of 65 and that many people with learning difficulties have remained under more stringent surveillance and have never had access to the 'ordinary life' that Alice eventually attained.

The question of rights and access to citizenship provides the focus for Tim Stainton's chapter. By examining the nature and content of debates surrounding both the passage of the Mental Deficiency Act in 1913 and attempts in the 1950s to reform the law, Tim suggests that the question of individual liberty and rights was central to both periods. Crucially, in the early twentieth century, concerns about the extent to which legislation constituted an attack on the rights of women and the working classes were imperiously ignored. The liberty of 'mental defectives' was sacrificed in the supposed interests of society. In the 1950s, however, the National Council for Civil Liberties exposed the inhumanity of the 'mental deficiency laws' and succeeded, at least in part, in changing the climate to one where there is a more general recognition that people with learning difficulties have the same human rights that we all expect.

Of course, the state has not been the only agent involved in caring for, and controlling, people with learning difficulties. In the nineteenth century, specific institutional provisions were more frequently provided by charitable bodies than by the state. Although the 1913 Act shifted the balance towards collectivist state intervention, charitable interest persisted. Indeed, as Jan Walmsley explores in Chapter 8, the Central Association for Mental Welfare and the National Association for the Parents of Backward Children both constituted important, albeit entirely distinct, elements of the political landscape of learning disability, straddling the boundary between public and private spheres. More particularly, Jan argues that the creation of the National Association in 1946 itself constituted a significant watershed in provision and was emblematic of a shift away from a rather abstract, paternalistic vision of 'doing good' towards a more concerted attempt by families of people with learning difficulties to assert their own rights.

People with learning difficulties and their families are not the only groups to have been ignored in academic accounts of the history of learning disability. As Duncan Mitchell argues in the next chapter, the role of nurses and other carers has also often been overlooked. While recognising that 'mental deficiency nurses' were part of a repressive regime responsible for elaborating and maintaining discipline, Duncan nevertheless points out that nurses themselves have occupied an ambiguous social and professional position. Sharing the same institutional space as the people for whom they were caring, and marginalised from the rest of the nursing profession, 'mental deficiency nurses' struggled to gain suitable recognition for their work. As Duncan suggests, if we are to understand how ideological and physical boundaries have been enforced in the past and if we are to comprehend fully how those boundaries have impacted on people's lives, then nursing history must be 'retrieved in parallel with that of people with learning difficulties'.

Crucially, for some people involved in the care of those with learning difficulties, the ambiguity of their position and the abuses that they witnessed together provided the inspiration for effecting change. In Chapter 10, Maureen Oswin recounts her own fearless efforts to improve the lives, and to fill 'the empty hours', of children with multiple disabilities in long-stay hospitals. Her harrowing account of institutional, administrative, and professional inertia, and of walls within walls, emphasises how difficult it can be to break down entrenched barriers. At the same time, Maureen's commitment offers a salutary reminder that courageous individuals can make an impact by challenging prejudice, neglect, and abuse.

From the 1970s, partly as a result of activists like Maureen Oswin, the political landscape of learning disability began to change. In line with developments in the treatment of the mentally ill, the large mental deficiency institutions that had darkened the twentieth-century skyline began a period of phased closure. People with learning difficulties began to cross the formidable boundary between the 'institution' and the 'community'. And yet this transition could be traumatic. As Mary Stuart's analysis of the experiences of women leaving a long-stay residential convent home shows, the success with which people cross boundaries between institutions and communities depends on a complex mix of social and personal factors. More critically, for some women the convent clearly offered more of a 'community' than the outside world.

In this context, it becomes imperative to prioritise the experiences of people with learning difficulties not only in recovering histories but also in elaborating policies. Of course, neither of these processes is easy, and both require collaborative efforts to breach the boundaries that can exist between people with learning difficulties, on the one hand, and researchers and practitioners with or without those difficulties, on the other. In the last chapter of the book, Dan Goodley not only examines the various ways in which self-advocacy can help to liberate the experiences of people with learning difficulties from the backwaters of historical awareness but also sets out ways in which constructing life-stories can encourage collaboration and challenge the hegemony of ideological, institutional, and political boundaries.

We hope that *Crossing Boundaries* serves to illustrate effectively how various boundaries have been formulated and crossed during the nineteenth and twentieth centuries. At the same time, by drawing analogies between the ways in which historical and current boundaries have been constructed, we hope that the book speaks directly to contemporary policy, professional, and personal issues. By integrating different accounts from researchers interested in disparate, but related, questions, the book is therefore intended not only to provide a descriptive account of how diverse boundaries have been breached in the past but also an illustration of the ways in which crossing disciplinary, political, intellectual, and personal boundaries can be fruitful, constructive and stimulating for a wide variety of audiences.

---

[1] The first conference, held in July 1997, was entitled 'Back to the Future? From Community to Institutions and Back Again'. The second, held in December 1997, was entitled 'Inclusion and Exclusion'.

Chapter 1

Researching our history: who is in charge?

Simone Aspis

Summary

In this chapter Simone Aspis explores the role of disabled people with learning difficulties in the research process. She also looks at the relationship between social research and social policy and the impact this has had on people's lives in the past and present. She challenges existing power relations, and the boundaries which exist, between non-disabled researchers and people involved in research who have been labelled as having learning difficulties, arguing that the latter need to have more control in setting the research agenda. In developing her arguments, she highlights the difficulties which she, as an individual, and organisations such as People First have experienced in gaining access to the funding which would enable them to cross the boundary between 'researched' and 'researcher'. She attributes these difficulties to the vested interests in maintaining the status quo.

I am an experienced disabled social researcher who has written extensively on issues which affect disabled people with learning difficulties. Recently, I have had papers published on self-advocacy, work and inclusive education. In addition I have undertaken research assignments into the needs of disabled people. During my time I have asked myself what are the roles of disabled people with learning difficulties in social research and what the impact is on our lives.

This became apparent when another disabled author asked me to write a chapter for a book about disabled people with learning difficulties. I was asked to write a chapter on the disabled people's movement and disabled people with learning difficulties. I decided to write a chapter explaining how the Disability Movement models the same social stratification in its own movement as it does in the outside society. After much discussion and apparent agreement I was somewhat surprised to be sent a letter from the editor saying, 'Perhaps my chapter would best be suited to a more practical book aimed at disabled people themselves.' The editor went on to say that it was too political for a book about disabled people with learning difficulties.

From the point of view of disabled people with learning difficulties it is very hard to take charge of what's written. It's never us who get the research contracts so we are never in charge of setting the agenda. Many social researchers in organisations, which are not controlled by disabled people with learning difficulties, pick disabled people with learning difficulties who have no knowledge of research or the issues which are trying to be addressed within the project. In this way they make sure the involvement of disabled people is only tokenistic. Disabled people with learning difficulties are subjects to be examined and picked around by non-disabled academics. We are never in the position to ask the questions. Instead we are used to prove non-disabled academics' hypotheses.

When disabled people with learning difficulties are included in research projects or as authors it's usually the 'tame' ones who are chosen. I am known to challenge, and I suspect people find me difficult to work with because I shake their assumptions and make life uncomfortable, so they tend to choose other people. I challenge the power relationship between non-disabled researchers and researchers who have been labelled by the education system as having learning difficulties.

The key area to address is who has the power to set the hypothesis, gather the evidence, interpret the experiences, make recommendations and define the political, physical and practical context. Social research is very important as a tool to influence social change and how this is carried out. Many of the Government policies are based on social research findings. It is not surprising that a lot of Government policies are confusing and ill-thought out in relation to disabled people with learning difficulties. This is because there are too many different researchers jumping on the bandwagon of learning disability research which includes providing their own interpretations and solutions to our individual and collective experiences.

The Government and research institutions have been very happy with these arrangements. Disabled people with learning difficulties are being used as puppets. This is left unchallenged, especially when organisations of disabled people with learning difficulties are on the whole unsuccessful in being funded to set out our own agendas and find our own solutions. As research is seen as a professional occupation with middle-class trappings it is not surprising that it is not in anyone's interest to give up power to people who do not have formal educational qualifications.

This is clearly highlighted by the way the Higher Education Funding Council (HEFC) funds colleges who are running higher education courses. Universities are funded for research according to the number of papers lecturers and researchers get published throughout the academic year. As people with learning difficulties like myself become more involved with research and the power which comes with it, the more the academics feel threatened by our presence. It always surprises me that disabled people with learning difficulties, who have no track record and have just been involved with research projects controlled by either non-disabled academics or research organisations for disabled people with learning difficulties, are those who always get invited to attend prestigious research conferences.

It's not a lot better in the disability research field, probably for the very same reasons, because disabled researchers have status and prestige and almost all have similar academic backgrounds to those who are not disabled people. Disabled people with learning difficulties are often overlooked when conferences on disability are being planned. I've challenged this on a number of occasions, only to be told that learning difficulties are being covered – but by researchers who don't have learning difficulties. This may account for the pre-occupation with 'the body' in disability research.[2] It's because people with bodily impairments dominate the disability movement that our issues don't get properly tackled or theorised.

Social research funding bodies are also part of the problem alongside HEFC. Maybe this is deliberate as major social research funding organisations provide funding for universities to carry out their research programmes, so there are cosy relationships. Whatever the reasons are they must be challenged and these institutions brought to account.

I know I am not the only disabled person with learning difficulties who has skills and who is not welcomed into the research field. The following is an example of how we are kept out.

A local People First group applied for some funding from a major grant-giving organisation to carry out some research into local service provision. The group had developed their own proposal. The funder asked the group to keep on reshaping the research proposal. They insisted that the group should have a non-disabled researcher, a request which was refused. The People First group contacted me and asked if I would like to assist on a consultancy basis. I was only too happy to assist. After hearing nothing for a long time I made contact with People First. I was surprised to learn that the grant-giving body had decided that the group was not established enough to carry out the research.

This is not the only People First group who were turned down because of wanting to carry out their research with the minimal interference of non-disabled academics and institutions. People First, London Boroughs, with an established disabled researcher had developed a bid for undertaking a major piece of work on direct payments. People First, London Boroughs had done all the campaign work on direct payments and ensured disabled people with learning difficulties were one of the groups who could receive direct payments.

Another organisation, controlled by non-disabled people, was awarded the grant. I wrote to the funder to find out why People First were not awarded the bid. Their representative said it was because the other organisation had more research experience. No consideration was given to the importance of disabled people carrying out their own research and the chicken and egg situation. Disabled people with learning difficulties could become experienced researchers if given the support and opportunities to do so. From my experience decent research takes time, and financial assistance is required not only in terms of expenses incurred but also being paid to do the job.

The question must be asked, what is everyone afraid of: their profession being deskilled and devalued, which may have an impact on the high status that social research has had? Opening up research, and encouraging people who are least intellectually valued to be outlining the agenda, could undermine the professional status research is given and thereafter the financial awards and social mobility which comes with it. For everyone involved in research it's not a price which anyone is willing to pay. As more disabled people, who are intellectually less valued, undertake jobs, the skills which are needed become less valuable and therefore attract lower wages. This is because, if disabled people with learning difficulties can do a job then it's open to the mass so therefore wages are depressed. And, on the other hand, any job which excludes the majority of people, but in particular people labelled as having learning difficulties, will be highly respected and highly paid and will only be open to the elite. In a capitalist state, where the divide between people who have and have not gained the learning experience on how to think, analyse and develop autonomous new ideas is increasing, so does the wage gap become bigger. It is therefore not in the research institution's interests to ensure the mass rather than the elite are able to benefit from undertaking autonomous research.

Is this the reason why the more experience I gain through submitting successfully published papers, the less research institutions and organisations want my expertise and skills?

---

2 B. Hughes, 'The Constitution of Impairment: Modernity and the aesthetics of oppression', *Disability and Society*, 14(2), (1999), 155-172.

Chapter 2

From community to institution – and back again

David Barron

Summary

In this autobiographical chapter, David Barron charts the course of his life. His theme is that while we must look forward to the present and future, we should not forget the past. In a moving and poignant account, David talks about his life in a series of institutions, and the physical and sexual abuse he experienced in them. His mission is to stop that happening to other children and young people, now and in the future.

I have been lecturing at universities, colleges and schools all over the country for the past fourteen years. I am asked the same questions over and over again, and the question is simply this – What gives me the strength to speak the way I do? My answer is that the strength that I have to speak is simply to help people who cannot speak for themselves.

In the eyes of God, be it he or she, we each and every one of us regardless of our abilities to do what we do or what we can't do, are all human beings. No one should look down on anybody else because of their disability, nobody should look down on somebody else and then look up to somebody else. It's one thing to change from using the word 'mental' to using 'people with learning difficulties', but it's not enough. One thing that must also change is that when they are speaking to the likes of us, including me, we must and they must start to look up and talk up to people and not down.

I'll illustrate this with an example. I was invited to go to Kent to take part in a study of child sexual abuse, which I experienced. We were shown photographs, some which I thought were utterly distasteful to show to anyone as a means to get the poor souls to show the way in which they had been sexually abused. I thought that was disgusting, the way they were doing it. They told those of us who took part that they were going to supply a booklet, and also an audio tape, but I have not seen or heard a dicky bird from any of it, and that was three years ago. The people that make these stories should have a right to have the story put their way, said their way without being altered; they should also have the right to have it in their possession at the end.

I myself am semi-illiterate and I'm not ashamed of that. I go round schools and colleges to give talks, I can read quite a bit of print, but to this day I cannot read a word of handwriting. So you see I've got my handicaps, they're there, but I was determined that I would fight on and I did my book[3] like young children do today in phonetic print.

My first boundary crossing – into foster care

I came out of an orphanage home at the age of three years. I was placed then to live with a foster mother whom I of course assumed was mother. What a lovely experience it must be for any man or any woman, anyone, to find they're suddenly going to meet up with a relative of someone whom they've never seen in their life. I personally was 'over the moon' as a child, but after the first few weeks with my mother, things were to change as quick as night changes to day, dark to light and vice versa. I came home from a nursery – I assumed it was a nursery anyway. The chair was pulled from underneath me and I went on to the b... floor, and I was still getting to the b... scullery – now I've had to change that because a lot of people said that they didn't know what a scullery was, well anybody from Yorkshire will. A scullery is the old kitchen of course. So the mangle top in the kitchen became my table, and then when it was bedtime I was thrown into the b... attic, and my mother always used the word 'b' for every sentence, so the attic floor became my bed, from three and a half years, the mangle top in the kitchen became the place where I had to have my food scraps if I was lucky, which meant I had to be going round knocking on people's doors asking for dry bread, shoving it in a carrier, shoving it up my jumper, and then going to school and eating it in the shed as a means of getting food, and I had to do this for quite a number of years.

I went to three special schools which, again, I notice they're now just dropping the name, the word 'special'. 'Special school' is no longer in existence. They're now saying they're going to put young people into – you know, join them up in big schools. The 'special' word has gone. I still love my mother. She's dead and buried. And it's my foster mother I'm referring to. So this went on for quite a long time. I would come home from school and when I came home from school I could guarantee it was either a beating first or later, but there was hardly any food. I had to be in the attic. This is going to embarrass you, but I can't help it. In those days, a lot of people know that in the old attics in the olden days these big houses – and they've still got them – they had manholes. Well, when I found that I was being forced and thrown into the attic at quarter to six on a night, and I wasn't even allowed to come out of it till the next day, you can quite appreciate when nature called there were problems. There were problems for me too when I was found out – because underneath the house where I lived they took in prison warders and one day the prison warder complained. He said there was a leak on his ceiling, but when they found out where the leak was coming from they made sure there was always a bucket left for me after that. Sorry, but I felt I had to say it.

As a means of getting food we had in the school where I went to, three schools. The first one you could buy soup, a penny a pot, ha'penny half a pot, and you could guarantee it was always burnt black. They made lovely pasties, and in those days if you threw one it would ricochet and come back. But nevertheless it was good as far as I was concerned. And so this is how it went on. The biggest part of the time was when it was half term. I run away from my sadistic foster mother because of cruelty, the severe beatings, a scald. One day I came home three minutes late from school. My foster mother firmly believed in beating first, questions after, one foot in the hearth, one out, and I got a pan of boiling scalding stock down my left leg with a scald which I'll carry with me to the grave. So all these things were there, but the love was still there for my foster mother. I still accepted these things.

I ran away from my foster mother's home, and I slept in a park, and it was only then I really knew the true value and love of young people. Today I will let no one come to me and say they are tearaways, they are layabouts; as far as I'm concerned I owe my life to the young people of yesteryear.

Boundary crossing two: into a mental institution

The next part I want to talk about is a mental institution. In this part I also bring in a theme. We must look forward to the present, but we must also remember the past.

Eventually I was taken away from my foster mother because a prison warder came in and saw that I was being beaten up in the back yard, and he intervened, and I was taken away from my foster mother's home at the age of eleven-and-a-half years for being severely beaten over and over and over again. He used to sneak food into the attic. He used to go, 'Mum's the word' – that was the only food I got. The people came with a search warrant – I didn't know what it was – but they came, and eventually after the to-and-froing with my foster mother and another – someone she'd taken off the street – I was taken away from her. The same night I was taken in to stay with children my age, but what they should have done is left me there, but no, the next day my foster mother appeared in Court. Great! She appeared in Court. I got a kick out of being in Court because seeing people walking round with wigs on, I thought they were Indians – but that was me as a child. Then things were to change. I was never ever to see my dear foster mother again alive. I was taken away by two burly men – I was told by these people … that just simply because I was being severely beaten up where a foster mother was being paid to look after me, practically starving me to death, that's why I was put in this mental hospital.

In the mental hospital it had its good points. It was spotless and clean, but I can always remember the day on one ward in particular, I will remember that day until I go to the grave, after they got the formalities out of the way and the forms were signed I was taken – this attendant took me with a big long dog chain to Ward 1. Ward 1 to me when I first went in of course, I just looked round. There was dear souls sat around the ward. The windows had bars on every one. The doors were locked. I was taken for a bath; they must have thought I couldn't bath myself, even that was locked, but from my experiences I know now why bath houses are locked. I settled in and I tried to communicate with the people – and I'll use that word again which I used earlier – 'poor souls'. I tried to communicate but couldn't because there was a big age gap, some twenty-odd years. Some of those poor souls must have been born practically in Whixley.

Figure 1 - Whixley Hospital

In Whixley you were not allowed to mix with the opposite sex. It was against the law throughout England, Scotland, Ireland and Wales that if a patient went out as a trustee it was all right for him to go and talk and mess about with his own sex but he must not go and be seen to talk – because I know from my documents – he must not go and be seen talking to a female because that's against the law, and that was the ruling and the law of the institutions at that time.

I'm now still back as a child, settled in, and we had a Superintendent there, and his voice became very familiar to me and it still is to this day; he came down to me and what did I cop? I got an occupation. I would go down, they would put me in the toilets, with a long corridor to scrub, to scrub the corridor, and when I'd finished start it over again, and the Superintendent came down and he said 'Hello David, you settling in all right, s'all right, ayh?' I got used to that word 'ayh' because that was his familiar saying, a posh word 'ayh', it came in all the time. Exercise – you had regular exercise, went out – but they also used the exercise yard as another thing.

Patients at that time, as we were called, if you did or said anything wrong, or you didn't please an attendant the way he wanted pleasing, he just put something in the Report Book and you were sent to Ward 1. Now Ward 1 was a notorious punishment ward. I as a child grew up and saw patients being brought into there for different things. One thing they had was the periodicals – privileges stopped. One of the main things I saw, was patients who smoked – I loved sweets, but I don't smoke, but they did, and they were desperate for getting cigarettes, so what they used to do they used to scoop dust off the floor just as a means of getting a sly smoke. A lot of those poor souls died with Yellow Jaundice, but it's a different wording medically in this book. Now, this was how it went on. I dreaded Ward 1 but nevertheless I was always in and out of there as I got older. I stayed in there, but I must admit it had its good points. If of course you did anything wrong, a patient would be sent out to scrub the concrete with a common house brick, half a bucket of cold water, regardless of the weather if it was freezing, and your ration of bread was cut from two slices of bread to half a slice of bread. If you pleased the attendants on the ward by going to bed with them, and all this kind of thing as it was done to me by force, well then brilliant! They'd give you maybe a little piece of extra bread, or something like that.

But let's look on the other side of the institution. It had its own tailor's shop, everywhere suits was made, mat shop, cobbler's shop, it had everything you could humanly think of in the institution, even to the laundry, everything was all under one roof.

The attendants had to have four qualifications: they had to know how to participate in sport; they had to have a form of religion whatever it was; they had to know how to use a bunch of keys; and they had to know how to use their fists. If they could do that they passed qualifications – there they were, they got the uniform, the lot. There was no male nurses in those days, only attendants. It wasn't all bad. We had one of the finest Scout bands throughout Yorkshire, and I used to love being in that. As I got older we used to go down to the village church once a month, and I used to brag being the youngest that our band was better than the ATC's band, and I am pleased to say that I'm still connected with some of the young people, who of course have now grown up, who lived in the village.

Figure 2 - The Scout Band

One thing I was taught in that institution was courtesy. Many a time when the telephone goes, if I'm speaking to someone I address that person as Madam she goes, 'I am no madam' – she maybe isn't. I don't know, well I said, 'It's how I've been brought up, Please Sir and Madam.'

Boundary crossing three: out of the institution

Coming out of the institution I was given a certification to certify I was sane but I found it very difficult because when I came out of Whixley, I had nowhere to go. I slept on the Town Hall steps, I slept at the back of the Leeds Parish Church in the Doss House because they did give me five pounds, and five pounds in those days went a long way.

Because of the indecent assaults by force against me I had three stigmas: one, that I had been in a mental hospital and nobody let me forget it, everywhere I went there was a finger pointing at me; secondly I could not read or write – to this very day I am still reasonably that way; thirdly I have to do something about sexual child abuse. Now I know in the eyes of God that it was wrong for me to attempt suicide, but I am sorry I did it because at the end I pulled through. Three times I attempted suicide because in my eyes any person that can go round the streets doing to children what they did to me and I mean me, not in turn those children growing up to be the same is wrong, and I thought then the only place I should be is six feet under, but you know, I did pull through.

I'd been in Pinderfield Hospital in Wakefield. On one occasion in those days if you attempted suicide you could be sent to prison for a long time. It was against the law to attempt to take your own life. It was a bigger offence than taking somebody else's, but for me, fortunately, I never got charged, I was sent to Pinderfield Mental Hospital in Wakefield. Eventually, though, that made no difference, the urges were still there, but finally the day came when I went and became a guinea-pig at Bridgewater Hospital. I had to get some solicitor who signed, and I was put on a drug called Stilboestrol. For three months I went through sheer hell until they got the right dosage and everything sorted itself out.

But do you know, I can hold my head up to the young, I can hold my head up to the old, and know full well as long as I live nothing will ever happen to any man, woman or child because I did something about it. It was a big battle.

---

[3] This refers to the book by David Barron, *A Price to be Born* (Mencap Northern Division 1996). Copies are available from Mencap Northern Division, 43 East Parade, Harrogate, North Yorkshire HG1 5LQ.

Chapter 3

Parallel stories

Dorothy Atkinson and Mabel Cooper

Summary

In this chapter, Dorothy Atkinson narrates the 'parallel stories' which have arisen from her work with Mabel Cooper. Not only do they write, and speak, in parallel but they also draw together the parallel stories of Mabel's life. There is the life story as Mabel told it from memory, and there are the different, sometimes conflicting, accounts of her life as told in the documentary records of the past. The two authors have crossed personal and social boundaries in order to work in partnership together. In finding out what happened to Mabel in the past, they have also begun to find out what happened, and how, to many other people with learning difficulties in years gone by.

Introduction

> *Years ago, if you wasn't married and you had a baby, that was*
> *a disgrace and they would say, 'Oh, the mother goes in a*
> *workhouse or a loony bin,' as they had in them days, or the*
> *mother went into a workhouse or a loony bin and the child was*
> *put into care.*[4]

This is an extract from 'Mabel Cooper's Life Story', an autobiographical account told entirely from memory. Interspersed with the memory of what happened to her, Mabel reflected on the meaning of her story and where it fitted into the wider social history of the time. The account above as to why there were more wards for women at St Lawrence's Hospital,[5] than there were for men, came to have a particular resonance for Mabel.

In her original account, quoted above, Mabel was making a general point about the fate in the past, of lone women and their illegitimate children. She later found, from her records, that this was her life too – she was just such a child, and she had ended up in care. And tragically, her mother had been labelled 'mental defective' and admitted to Darenth Park Hospital, a long stay institution in Kent. In her reflective statement, Mabel had unknowingly previewed the reality of her own life. When she spoke those original words she knew nothing of her early history. That came later in her quest to find out the missing bits of her story. Now there are two parallel stories: one told by Mabel, from memory, and another one, that is being gradually revealed from her records. Each story is further confirmed or contradicted by family memories.

We reflect on those stories in this chapter, on how and why they were told, and what they mean. But there is another parallel story running through the chapter itself, which is told through the different voices of its two authors. We worked together on compiling this chapter. We worked, as Mabel puts it, as 'partners', planning, preparing and reviewing it together at every stage – until the final one. The telling of the story together proved to be a task even beyond partnership. So the story is told in parallel – through the spoken words of Mabel, and through my written words. It is still Mabel's story, but it is compiled from a variety of sources and my written words are intended to bring the pieces together and help put them into context. In the end, though, it is Mabel's words which count, and which will be remembered long after mine have been forgotten.

The need to know

In telling her original story from memory, Mabel crossed a major boundary. She had been, for much of her life, a victim of a set of historical circumstances and events which had seen many people – like herself – excluded from everyday life in long-stay institutions.

In recent years, she has become instead a historical witness, an eye-witness of an era fast disappearing. In her life story, Mabel describes what happened to her, and how she crossed other boundaries throughout her life: from children's homes to the 'mental deficiency' system; from institutional to community care; from ex-patient to self-advocate, and the person she is now, able to represent herself and others. Mabel's capacity to tell her story, and to reflect on it, has enabled her to understand what happened to her, and to challenge it.

It also prompted her to ask many more questions about herself, her life and her identity, for example: Who was she? Who were her parents? What had become of them? She could remember living in a children's home in Bedford, but did not know how or why she came to be there. She remembered more than 20 years of living in St Lawrence's but, again, she did not know how or why she came to be incarcerated there nor why she was there for so long.

Mabel's need to know led her into a quest for documentary evidence from her own case records and from the archived records of the institutions where she spent her childhood and much of her adult life. Such a quest proved daunting at times, and some of the language of the past was hurtful, but the need to know proved a strong driving force. The quest took Mabel and me to view her case notes at the offices of the Lifecare Trust (on the site of St Lawrence's) and to visit the London Metropolitan Archives and the Bedfordshire County Records office.

Mabel thus became engaged in historical research, a process which proved to be fascinating and hurtful. In taking on the role of researcher, Mabel crossed another boundary, as she explains:

> *There's so much I didn't know that I'm finding out now.
> I went to St Lawrence's [the location of the Lifecare
> Trust] and I went to the archives. Some of it, like the
> names they called you in them days, hurt a little bit but
> otherwise I thought it was great. It was something I
> needed to find out. And going to the archives, that
> was great again, that was somewhere I've never been,
> and I enjoyed it.*[6]

The search was revealing. It revealed the names used in the past, many of which have now passed into everyday use as terms of abuse. It was a salutary moment for Mabel to find in her records that such terms had been applied to her younger self. And yet it remains her overriding view that it is 'great' to know about oneself, and to know about the past – in spite of the words used and the messages they conveyed. This is because Mabel, and other people with learning difficulties, have been excluded from their own life-stories. She, together with many other people who have lived in long-stay institutions, have had little if any access to, or knowledge of, their prior lives.

Parallel stories, parallel lives

Mabel and I met in 1994 when I was looking for life stories for inclusion in the Open University course (then in preparation), 'Working as Equal People'. We met by chance, and talked on the train home of Mabel's long-held wish to tell her story. We might have met – but luckily did not – in the early 1970s when, by chance, I was employed as a Mental Welfare Officer in Croydon, Surrey, and Mabel was a long-stay resident in St Lawrence's Hospital in nearby Caterham. In those days Mabel was on the inside of a social divide, and I was on the outside, patrolling the very boundary which demarcated her life. Our worlds have both changed in ways hitherto unthinkable. The changes in policy and practice which enabled Mabel to move from long-stay resident to community living, citizenship, self-advocacy and, latterly, historical research and writing, have enabled me to move from the gatekeeping and boundary patrols of the 1970s to being an oral historian and researcher in the 1990s. Between us, we crossed many boundaries in order to take up our joint work on the history of learning disability.

Our first task was the writing of Mabel's story from memory. We met at her home for this purpose, where she talked to me about her childhood in a children's home, her move to St Lawrence's Hospital and her later life in the community, including her work in the self-advocacy movement. We tape-recorded our conversations and I transcribed them word for word in question-and-answer, conversational format. That formed the basis of a more flowing narrative account which I prepared and then read back to Mabel for confirmation or amendment. The readings triggered more memories which were themselves incorporated into the unfolding story. The result was initially a private publication for Mabel and her friends, but subsequently the story was published in a book.[7]

This story, as indicated above, was incomplete. It led to our next task: to unearth from personal and public records the bigger picture of Mabel's life – those parts which she had never known, and those which she had forgotten. Our starting point, as Mabel indicated earlier, was the Lifecare Trust, where her personal case notes were housed. She remembers that momentous visit:

> *I went with Dorothy to St Lawrence's, and Gloria came
> [her close friend], and we went up, and we had a look. They
> said we could look through their records, my records, and
> they were very nice to us. We sat in a little room for ages, it
> was 12 o' clock when we stopped, and then we asked could I
> take some of them away, that I would like some of them.
> They said to me, 'The ones you want you put on one side,
> and the ones you don't want put on the other side.' The
> ones I didn't want were not about the family, and they're
> not about anything that would interest people outside. I
> put to one side everything about me and my family.*[8]

In the life story told from memory, Mabel said that she had no family and was placed in a children's home in Bedford which was run by nuns. Later on, following a test at County Hall, she was admitted, still only a child, to St Lawrence's Hospital:

> *I moved to St Lawrence's when I was seven because they
> only took children who went to school in this home. And I
> never went to school in this home. And I never went to school
> so I had to move. In them days they give you a test before*

*they make you go anywhere. It used to be a big place, all
full of offices and what have you, because they said you
should be able to read when you're seven or eight. I
couldn't read. I hadn't been to school. That was 1952, I
was seven years old.*[9]

The case records we consulted told a related but different story. It
was true, Mabel was placed as a child at a children's home in
Bedford. We now know its name, St Etheldreda's, and the dates
when Mabel lived there. But St Etheldreda's turned out to be just
one of a whole series of children's homes in which Mabel had spent
her childhood: Easneye Nursery; Stowlangtoft; Ashford; Mariston
House; and Hutton Residential School. These were lost from memory.
Only St Etheldreda's remained intact:

*When I was little I lived in another place like St
Lawrence's, but it was just for children. This was in Bedford.
It used to be run by nuns. And that had bars up at the
windows as well, because they used to call them places
madhouses. It was in Bedford. They haven't got it any
more, they've vanished it.*[10]

For much of her young life Mabel thought she had no family. She
then found she had an aunt, and made contact with her. At the time
of our visit to read her St Lawrence's case notes, Mabel had no idea
of the circumstances of her admission into the child care system.
The case notes revealed a tragic story: a mother found begging on
the streets of London, with her four week old baby in her arms, was
deemed to be 'feeble-minded', and was admitted to Darenth Park
Hospital. This was Mabel's mother. They were parted when Mabel
was a month old, and their paths never crossed again. The child
care system took over Mabel's life, and she started the institutional
round which was to take her across four counties and through six
homes, until, herself labelled as 'feeble-minded', she was admitted
to St Lawrence's Hospital in 1957.

The language and labels were hurtful for me to read out, and for
Mabel to hear. They were, in any case, later contested by one of
Mabel's distant cousins who knew her mother years ago. In a dramatic
exchange at the 'Back to the Future' conference held at the Open
University in 1997, some of the unknown information was disclosed
publicly to Mabel at the end of her presentation:

Mabel: *I don't think my family did anything wrong. My mum may have rebelled, I don't know, but that doesn't give them the right to put her away, where the police put her. I don't know much about it.*

Marjorie: *I'll tell you, Mabel. You had a Victorian grandfather, so if anyone stepped out of line, as your mother stepped out of line, though not in any way which we would think so in these days of course. But in those days it was different, and that's where it all started. Your grandfather, I'm afraid, was the culprit. He threw your mother out. He made you into paupers. He was in many ways a good man, but he didn't recognise what he was doing.*

Mabel: *Marjorie knows a lot about the family, and she tells me bits that no one else in the family have tried to do.*

Marjorie: *I want to contradict one of the things that was said in the records about your mother, Mabel, that she was thought to be an imbecile. She wasn't. She was a very, very normal intelligent girl that had a high education, and there wasn't anything like that about her.*[11]

Making sense of history

Although she did not know it at the time, Mabel was admitted to St Lawrence's Hospital under the terms of the 1913 and 1927 Mental Deficiency Acts. It was only through our search for her recorded history that she found this out. It was the terminology of this legislation which 'hurt a bit', a point she made again when we talked about our visit to the Lifecare Trust:

I was shocked only by the names I was called, and for the places they'd put me in, and from where I'd been expelled. I didn't know that. It shocked me, and I think it makes you different if you know that, it makes you harder than you would be normally.

The case records told us much of what had happened to Mabel, and when, and where she had ended up. As stated earlier, St Lawrence's was the end point of a process which had started in infancy. Moved around from pillar to post, excluded from school and labelled unteachable, by the time she was tested at County Hall, London, Mabel was declared 'practically illiterate'. Not only that, but the house mother from her most recent children's home (her sixth placement) said she was 'excitable and childish ... and takes time to settle'. No allowances were made for a history of loss, deprivation, and change, or for the absence of any family or home life. Described later in her hospital case notes as timid and shy, and said to speak little, Mabel's own account of institutional life was of adopting a policy of deliberate silence. This was a form of protest about what had happened to her, as she made clear in our work together on this chapter:

> *I never said anything in the hospital because there was no point. Nobody listened, so why speak? If you spoke they told you to shut up, so I stopped saying anything. I didn't talk, it was a protest really rather than anything else. I only said two words, 'yes' and 'no', and mostly I only said 'no'!*

The hospital records did not – and could not – account for Mabel's silence. They recorded only that she was quiet. Elsewhere they catalogued the names and dates of events but were not able to say why these events occurred. It is the question 'why?' which is the most haunting one to arise from our search into historical records, and for which there is no answer. The course of Mabel's life is now largely charted, but she still does not know why she was made to take that course – a point we returned to again in preparing this chapter:

> *We found out some of the bits I wanted to know, but some of it is not in the records. It tells you what happened to mum and me but it doesn't tell you why. I didn't know anything about mum because Aunt Edie always kept me apart from the rest of them, and I never saw any of them till she died.*

> *It's great what we've found out, but what I'd really love to find out is why I was separated? Why did mum get put in hospital when she had a child to look after? She probably would have stayed if she could. Why did they separate us? OK, so mum was*

*begging, well people still do that nowadays but their
children don't get put in care.*

*I'd love to know why. It's very unfair really. Mum didn't
have any say in it, and it's wrong. Why were we
separated? Mum hadn't done a crime or anything. If I'd
known where mum had gone I would have gone looking, but
it's taken me over 50 years to get this far. And we asked just
in time because my records were just about to be thrown out.*

Mabel's story is important to her. Knowing about the past, hurtful
though it may be, is better than not knowing – even if the central
question 'Why?' remains unanswerable. This is because Mabel's
story has a significance wider than that of a single autobiography.
It is one story among many, actual and potential, which between
them will begin to tell much of the history of learning disability
from the point of view of the people so labelled. Mabel is aware of
the social and historical significance of her story and the stories of
others. Part of her mission now is to encourage other people to tell
their stories and to teach practitioners, researchers and historians
how to listen and to learn from them:

*My story and a lot more will help people with a learning
difficulty, and I hope it will learn them to tell their story of
what happened to them. Other people too can learn from
it like the people who came to our workshop in Kent [for
practitioners]. They learn what things went on all those
years and they learn to change: they listen and learn.*

*It's not just my story and what happened to me, it happened
to loads of people, it even happened to Gloria [a close friend].
It happened to my mum though she ran away and never
went back.*

*I'm involved in People First, I'm chair of Croydon People
First. Before that I was chair of London People First, for
four years, helping people with learning difficulties to speak
up: enabling people to speak up, and educating other people
to make that happen. Now I'm encouraging other people to
tell their stories. I think it's good, and I think it teaches the
public that people with learning difficulties are not going*

*to hurt anyone and all the time we can get people to write
their story and tell what happened to them, and publish it,
or do a book for themselves – like Doris [a friend] wants to
do – then it helps everyone. And Doris wants to show her
book to other people, when it's done, so she can say, 'Look,
this is what I've done, and this is what it's all about.'*

Conclusion

The children's home in Bedford has been 'vanished'. Most of St
Lawrence's Hospital has now gone. The walls and buildings that for
124 years defined and contained the lives of thousands of people
have come down. The old nurses' home, the one remaining fragment of
the institution which remains on the site, will also disappear when
the Lifecare Trust moves into new offices.

And then what? Who will remember, and regret, what happened to
Mabel Cooper and other people with learning difficulties, who lived
in St Lawrence's and the numerous other institutions throughout
the country? Many – though by no means all – have crossed the
boundary from institutional to community living. In her life, Mabel
has shown that that was just one boundary among many which had
to be crossed. For her, it was not enough to live in the community;
it was also important to have a say, and to be listened to; becoming
a self-advocate made that possible. And now 'speaking up' has led
her to tell her story first from memory and then from records, and
to make sense of the parallels and differences.

The telling of her story has enabled Mabel to understand, and
reflect on, the individual and social circumstances which have
shaped her own experiences, and to see them in a wider, historical
context. The more stories told, according to Mabel, the better educated
the public becomes, and the more is revealed of the history of learning
disability.

When the walls of the institutions have come down, and there is
nothing left in the landscape to show what once was there, it is the
stories which will endure. This is why the telling, writing and pre-
serving of history is so important, as Mabel explains:

What's left of St Lawrence's, the Lifecare offices, is going to go. That's a good thing. But it's important that the books stay because that's a reminder of what's happened. Even if anything happened to me, the books must stay. And my records, they must be kept safe, I don't want anything to happen to them.

---

4 Mabel Cooper, 'Mabel Cooper's Life Story', in Atkinson, D., Jackson, M. and Walmsley, J., *Forgotten Lives: Exploring the History of Learning Disability,* Kidderminster: BILD Publications 1997, p29.

5 St Lawrence's Hospital, Caterham, in Surrey.

6 Mabel Cooper, 'My Quest to Find Out', in Atkinson, D., McCarthy, M., Walmsley, J., Cooper, M., Rolph, S., Aspis, S., Barette, P., Coventry, M. and Ferris, G. *Good Times, Bad Times: Women with Learning Difficulties Telling their Stories.* Kidderminster: BILD Publications 2000.

7 This refers to 'Mabel Cooper's Life Story' (see Note 4 above).

8 Extract from 'Mabel Cooper's Life Story', p. 22.

9 Extract from 'Mabel Cooper's Life Story', p. 22.

10 Extract from 'Mabel Cooper's Life Story', p. 22.

11 This extract is taken from the video transcript of the conference 'Back to the Future', held at the Open University in July 1997.

Chapter 4

Understanding segregation from the nineteenth to the twentieth century: re-drawing boundaries and the problems of 'pollution'

Lindsay Brigham

Summary

In this chapter Lindsay Brigham explores how learning disability was understood in late nineteenth- and early twentieth-century Britain and the extent to which people with learning difficulties came to be seen as a threat to society. She looks at the question of why women with learning difficulties, in particular, became a focus of concerns about immorality and fecundity and a target for policies which attempted to control their sexuality. In addressing these issues she maps out the changing social, political and economic context and the re-drawing of boundaries between classes, 'races', men and women, normality and abnormality and the public and private domains. The idea of 'pollution' is related to the crossing of these boundaries.

Introduction

In Chapter 3, Mabel Cooper describes her quest to discover her past. In Mabel's search she finds documentary evidence from her own case records as well as archived records of the institutions with which she came into contact. In the role of historian, Mabel finds out how she was separated from her mother when she was only a month old. Her mother was labelled as 'feeble-minded' and admitted to a mental institution and Mabel entered the child-care system. This powerful account reveals the benefits to Mabel of finding out about her past and how things were, but she is left with the unanswered question of why.

> *It's great what we've found out, but what I'd really like to find out is why I was separated? Why did mum get put in hospital when she had a child to look after ... I'd love to know why. It's very unfair really. Mum hadn't done a crime or anything. ('Mabel Cooper', Chapter 3)*

The aim of this chapter is to attempt to address the question, 'why?' Why did women like Mabel's mother, who had a child outside marriage, frequently become labelled, institutionalised and denied basic human rights? To search for the answer it is necessary to go back even further than Mabel's search, to the nineteenth century.

To begin the search some understanding of how mental impairment[12] or 'idiocy' was constructed in the nineteenth century is needed. I provide this background, firstly, by giving a brief introduction to the changing economic, social and political context and, secondly, by exploring the cultural and symbolic terrain. In exploring the latter, the key theme will be re-drawing and crossing boundaries; not in the geographical sense, as charted by a map, but boundaries of classification – between 'races', men and women, civilisation and nature, public and private, human and animal. Mary Douglas has argued, that to understand any culture it is necessary to look at the total structure of its classifying symbols.[13] If classification systems establish boundaries, these lines can also be transgressed, and it is these crossings which she associates with ideas of 'pollution'.

> *..the only way in which pollution ideas make sense is in reference to a total structure of thought whose key-stone,*

> *boundaries, margins and internal lines are held in relation by rituals of separation.*[14]

To understand 'idiocy' in the nineteenth century context, it is necessary to examine these ideas about 'pollution' and the extent to which this marginalised group of people came to be seen as dangerous and a threat to society. To complement Douglas's structuralist framework of analysis, I also draw upon the concept of discourse[15] to explore how sets of ideas about 'femininity' and 'idiocy' were interwoven.

The nineteenth century context

The nineteenth century has been classified as a period of industrialisation that involved far-reaching changes in social, political and economic organisation and impacted upon people's lives in a myriad of ways. Key features of industrialisation were the movement of population from rural settings to towns and cities and associated changes in work patterns; the move away from agriculture, and work centred round the home, to work in factories and, to a lesser extent, offices. Alongside this was the discipline of fixed hours of work, increasing mechanisation, where machines drove the pace of work, and division of labour. Demographically, it was accompanied by population growth with the growing urban population being fed by the declining population who remained in agriculture, and the new sources of cheap food from the expanding number of colonies, acquired as Britain was consolidating its empire.[16] Overall, individuals were moving from being independent producers to waged labourers; they were selling their labour to those who owned the means of production (factories, machinery, capital) who in turn sold the commodities produced for a profit. The revolutionary aspect was not so much an increase in production per se but the radical changes in the way that production took place.

However, this was an uneven process of development. For example, Lancashire has been described as the birthplace of the industrial revolution. From the late eighteenth to the early twentieth century the economy of the north west was largely built upon the increasingly mechanised cotton industry. According to the 1841 Census, over a third of the people in this area worked in the textile industry alone and, nationally, less than a quarter worked in agriculture and related activities.[17] Industrialisation was a social process and like all social processes it took place over a period of time, with some regions being affected much earlier than others.

Politically, the period was characterised by an extension of franchise, the growth of a working class and a rising class of industrialists and manufacturers who were consolidating their power base, often in conflict with the traditional authority of the older land-owning class. This transition was a time of instability and uncertainty and the 1830s and 1840s saw strong challenges to the emerging new order from Chartists, Radicals, Luddites and early Trade Unionists.[18]

The social implications of changes in the way that production took place were far reaching and had a specific effect on women. Prior to industrialisation, production had largely taken place in the private domain of the home (i.e. the family could be seen as the economic unit of production), and women had played a large part in both agriculture and the production of textiles. During industrialisation there was an increasing separation of 'work' from the daily routines of domestic life as the factory replaced the home as the economic unit of production.[19] As the century progressed, women and children were increasingly excluded from the public domain of paid work[20] and confined to the private domain of unpaid work in the home and family. However, this process was also geographically uneven and there were significant class differences. For example, 'The great importance of the female labour force in cotton gave [working-class] women in Lancashire more economic independence than anywhere else in the country.'[21] Despite the economic realities and experiences of many women, it has been argued that it was during the nineteenth century that the idealised role of housewife and associated ideology of domesticity was born.[22]

Although less well documented, there were also many changes for people who were physically or mentally impaired. The new discipline of the factory system with its emphasis on speed, timekeeping and production norms proved a hostile environment for people with impairments.[23] It has been argued that this meant an exclusion of disabled people from the production process. Whereas they had been able to make some contribution to agriculture or small-scale industry, they effectively became disabled by this new form of organisation of work. It is important not to idealise the pre-industrial era as a golden age for people with physical and mental impairments but it has been argued that increasing pressures of industrialisation on the family unit made it less likely that families would be able to support an additional non-productive member. For 'idiots' who were not supported by families, the workhouse, prison or asylums for the insane were their most likely destinations. However, despite the general trend towards specialised asylums in the nineteenth century,[26] asylums for 'idiots' were still a rarity and, by the end of the nineteenth century, statistics show that the number of people defined as 'idiots' in public institutions in 1881 had risen to 29,452 – of these only three percent were in specialised institutions.[27]

In general, the burgeoning growth of asylums reflected the trend towards segregation of those who could not or would not conform to the discipline of new patterns of work. Breakdown in traditional means of authority associated with the industrial revolution, and the political instability that accompanied this, led to concerns on the part of the rising bourgeoisie of social unrest.[28] Asylums can be seen as having both a repressive and an ideological function in terms of social control[29] and served as a means of classifying and segregating the 'normal' from the 'abnormal': those who couldn't work from those who wouldn't work; the 'deserving' from the 'undeserving' poor. The result for the mentally impaired and other groups, those who were poor or old and dependent, was institutionalisation. Being mentally impaired was increasingly defined as a social problem but so was pauperism and both became associated with notions of immorality, degeneration and criminality.

The nineteenth century can be summed up as period of economic, political and social change that had an impact upon all groups in society. Whereas women were increasingly segregated in the private institution of the family, people who were physically or mentally impaired were increasingly segregated in the public institutions of the workhouse or asylum. The nineteenth century can therefore be seen as a time for the re-drawing of boundaries between classes, between masculinity and femininity, between public and private, and between normality and abnormality.

Changing classifications

The nineteenth century was characterised not only by a revolutionary change in its structure but also in its ideas. Previous dominance by religious ideas had gradually, since the eighteenth century, become overtaken by a new faith in the power of science to solve problems, classify and explain the natural and social world. This 'age of reason' provided the context for scientific thinking to flourish and one of the key European thinkers of the nineteenth century was Charles Darwin. His book, *The Origin of Species*, provided a challenge to the religious discourses on the existence of man by proposing that man had evolved from lower organisms by adaptation to environmental conditions through hereditary mechanisms. His ideas were quickly seized upon and applied to society, resulting in forms of Social Darwinism dominating the late nineteenth- and early twentieth-century intellectual scene. Social Darwinism in turn became equated with eugenic beliefs and practices. A cousin of Darwin, Francis Galton, provided the missing link between Darwin's thinking and eugenics.[30] To quote Galton:

> *My general object has been to take note of the varied hereditary faculties of different men, and of the great differences in different families and races, to learn how far history may have shown the practicability of supplanting inefficient human stock by better strains, and to consider whether it might be our duty to do so by such efforts as may be reasonable, thus exerting ourselves to further the ends of evolution more rapidly ...*
>
> *Its intention is to touch on various topics more or less connected with that of cultivation of race, or, as we might call it with 'eugenic' questions.*[31]

As well as eugenic ideas relating to the 'improvement of the race' there was also a set of ideas in which, 'science purported to demonstrate not only the number and characteristics of each 'race', but also a hierarchical relationship between them.'[32] These racist assumptions must be placed in the context of Britain at a time of consolidation of empire and exploitation of colonies. To justify the subjugation and control of other people within a religious framework, which stressed that 'all men were equal', people in the colonies were defined as sub-human, as 'other'.[33]

Representations of 'idiocy' were interrelated with classifications of 'race' in several ways. Firstly, medical texts frequently likened 'idiots' to more 'primitive' people.[34] The original Langdon-Down classification was based on racist assumptions and identified a sub class of 'idiots' as 'mongolian', thus equating 'idiocy' with a 'race' further down the evolutionary hierarchy (see Chapter 5). Ideas about the evolutionary superiority of the white 'race' led to concerns to maintain and improve the lead over more 'primitive' races and hence to eugenic concerns about curtailing the fertility of the 'unfit'. The 'unfit' included people with mental impairments and, as concerns about differential fertility rose, it also included what were seen as undesirable elements of the working classes.[35] As Douglas has argued:

> *No particular set of classifying symbols can be understood*
> *in isolation, but there can be hope of making sense of them*
> *in relation to the total structure of classifications in the*
> *culture in question.*[36]

Classifications of 'race', class and mental impairment are all inter-related here and 'idiocy' can be seen in terms of ambiguities and hence potential 'pollution'. Douglas identifies four kinds of social pollution that represent danger and threat: danger pressing on external boundaries; danger from transgressing the internal lines of the system; danger in the margins of the lines; and danger from internal contradictions.[37] Concerns about curtailing the 'fertility of the unfit' can be understood as an external boundary issue concerning the overall 'improvement of the race'. Langdon-Down's classification can be understood in terms of 'idiots' transgressing internal lines between 'races' and, as a marginalised group, being on the margin of the lines. In other words, 'people who are left out of the patterning of society, who are placeless',[38] who are not seen as quite human, yet not animal. Interestingly, Douglas focuses her analysis on what she refers to as 'primitive cultures' and their systems of religious beliefs. The nineteenth century was a period where scientific discourses were beginning to compete with and dominate religious discourses, yet ideas about pollution and taboo are equally relevant.

An example of the fourth strand of pollution is the internal contra-dictions in categorising mental impairment itself. Some of the first specialist schools were characterised by a humanitarian approach towards 'idiots' and stressed their educability. An asylum for 'idiots' was founded in Highgate in 1847 under royal patronage and the brochure for the asylum stated that, 'It may now be pronounced, not as an opinion, but as a fact, a delightful fact, that THE IDIOT MAY BE EDUCATED.'[39] This pronouncement was being made not only in England but in Europe and America and from 1837 Edouard Séguin had been a pioneer in the field of training and education for people classified as 'idiots'.[40] Séguin's ideas linked into broader religious discourses and the schools he established could be seen in terms of refuges or sanctuaries from an uncaring world. He saw the 'idiot' as closer to nature, somehow more distanced and less corrupted by the artificiality of culture and therefore possessing an inherent goodness and moral wisdom, a 'minor, legally irresponsible, isolated without associations, a soul shut up in imperfect organs, an innocent'.[41] This relates to Wolfensberger's categorisation of social roles[42] and conjures up ideas of the 'holy innocent' or 'eternal child'. However, above all, Séguin emphasised the educability of 'idiots'. This illustrates that ideas about mental impairment were not contained within one nation and culture but crossed national boundaries.

Towards the latter part of the nineteenth century these attitudes, shaped by religious discourses, gradually became replaced (or co-existed) with notions of the 'idiot' as subhuman, an object of fear and dread and a 'threat to society'. Drawing upon scientific discourses, more emphasis was placed on determinism via hereditary factors rather than the potential for development through education. Samuel Howe argued that:

> *Idiots form one rank of that fearful host which is ever pressing upon society with its suffering, its miseries and its crimes and which society is ever trying to hold off at arm's length, – to keep in quarantine, to shut up in jails and almshouses, or, at least to treat as a pariah cast; but all in vain.*[43]

The Royal Commission on the Care of the Feeble-Minded (1904-1908) mirrored these sentiments by arguing that it was necessary to 'control this wandering population of mentally defective persons, who are many of them dangerous, morally and physically, and criminal in their characteristics.'[44] These quotations emphasise the need to segregate and control, or reinforce boundaries against 'pollution'. Reference to criminality potentially broadens the notion of 'pollution' to other groups such as the criminal elements within the working class.

In terms of classification, women had been represented in oppositional terms, or as 'other', to men and also became a focus for concerns about pollution. Williams has described converging discourses of 'race', gender, and learning disability[45] and this is illustrated in the following quote from Darwin:

> *Woman seems to differ from man in mental disposition*
> *chiefly in her greater tenderness and less selfishness ...*
> *It is generally admitted that with woman the powers*
> *of intuition, of rapid perception, and perhaps of imitation,*
> *are more strongly marked than in man; but some, at*
> *least, of these faculties are characteristic of the lower*
> *races, and therefore of a past and lower state of civilisation.*[46]

Regarding sexuality, there are interesting parallels between 'race' and 'idiocy'. Prior to the nineteenth century women had often been portrayed as overtly sexual. This could be linked to religious beliefs about Adam's temptation by Eve and the resulting Fall, but in the nineteenth century there was an effective de-sexing of women to emphasise their difference to men and inherent morality. In a similar way to Séguin's portrayal of 'idiots', women were seen as untainted by the public world, closer to nature than culture. Earlier representations of sexualised women have their parallel in representations of 'race' where both sexes are portrayed as having a hidden but dangerous sexuality.[47] Similarly, with 'idiocy', there are discourses which emphasise sexuality and fertility. The superintendent of the Massachusetts School for the Feeble-Minded wrote in 1912:

> *Feeble-minded women are almost invariably immoral and*
> *if at large usually become carriers of disease or give*
> *birth to children who are as defective as themselves. The*
> *feeble minded woman who marries is twice as prolific as the*
> *normal woman.*[48]

This locked into the more general eugenic concern about differential fertility between classes but the convergence of discourses about 'femininity' and 'idiocy' meant that 'feeble-minded' woman in particular had become a focus for concerns about 'pollution'.

Public and private

The changing situation of women in the dramatic upheavals of the nineteenth century has sometimes been referred to as the 'Woman Question'. In the pre-industrial era it has been argued that women's role was unproblematic; it was under the control of an all-pervasive patriarchal authority and was seen as part of a grand order ultimately prescribed by God.[49] With the development of modern industrial capitalism, and the division between public and private domains, men were demoted to wage earners and, in principle, there was nothing to stop women from adopting this role as well (albeit at lower wages and with a more circumscribed range of jobs to choose from). Indeed, an increasing number of women were self supporting. In the 1851 Census, 42% of women between the ages of 20 and 40 were identified as unmarried, prompting W. R. Greg, a liberal manufacturer, to state that it was:

> *A number quite disproportionate and quite abnormal ...*
> *proportionally most numerous in the middle and upper*
> *classes – who have to earn their own living, instead of*
> *spending and husbanding the earnings of men ...*
> *[those] who remain unmarried constitute the problem*
> *to be solved, the evil and anomaly to be cured.*[50]

This quotation has to be understood in the context of the time where boundaries between private/public and feminine/masculine were being redrawn and the dominant set of ideas in relation to women emphasised domesticity and their role as 'housewives'. The private domain or home became associated with the more human values of personal contact, nurturing and affection, values antithetical to the public world of work and the economy governed by the impersonal laws of the market – competition and profit. The 'private' therefore represented an older form of morality and spirituality, values which became associated with 'femininity', whereas the 'public' represented the more aggressive values of 'survival of the fittest' associated with 'masculine rationalism'.[51] The 'evil' and 'anomaly' referred to by Greg related to women crossing the line between private and public, thus disrupting the classification order and becoming a potential pollutant or as Douglas would say, 'matter out of place'.

In society as a whole, the new schism between public and private domains and the construction of woman's morality and spirituality was articulated around ideas of 'Englishness'. It meant that Britain could present a morally superior image to the world and simultaneously operate a market economy that did not count the casualties. Poovey has argued that what was being consolidated was middle-class power and that, 'the domestic ideal was a crucial component in a series of representations that supported both the middle class's economic power and its legitimation of this position.'[52]

Who was to blame?

It is in this context that discourses of blame concerning the 'problem of idiocy' must be understood. The following quotation from Séguin reveals his anxieties pertaining to the transgression of the private/public boundary:

> *Intellectual or business excitement has taken possession*
> *of both sexes, a young woman with a child has to contend*
> *with social difficulties, as if she were not engaged in a*
> *labour which requires all the resources of her constitution.*[53]

The implications of this type of thinking were that a woman could not participate in both the world of intellectual and business stimulation and look after a child; to aspire to the domestic ideal she must renounce all else. Furthermore, if she transgressed boundaries while pregnant the penalties were an increased risk of producing an 'idiot child':

> *We overburden women ... they overburden themselves*
> *and choose or accept burdens unfit for them ... as*
> *soon as women assumed the anxieties pertaining to*
> *both sexes they gave birth to children whose like*
> *had hardly been met with thirty years ago.*[54]

This relates to the previous discussion of the 'woman question' – to maintain the stability of the new order with the separation of public and private spheres, it was essential that the opposition between men and women was maintained. Ironically, in referring to 'anxieties' Séguin assumed that women, in a romanticised past, were free of any burdens and effectively masked the extent of their participation in production. Discourses of blame, such as this one, acted as warnings about what would happen if women stepped outside their 'natural' role and relate to ideas about pollution in two ways: firstly women have crossed internal lines and secondly they have produced children who were seen as polluting the 'race'.

A rather different strand of the woman-blaming theme relates more specifically to the boundaries of women's physical bodies. One type of pollution belief was related to bodily emissions which crossed the external boundaries of the body and menstruation carried a particularly potent taboo. Séguin states that one condition particularly conducive to the production of an 'idiot child' is if the woman, 'has conceived at a time when spermatozoa have encountered noxious fluids of venereal or menstrual origin.'[55]

Venereal disease also interacted with pollution beliefs in a different way. The mid-nineteenth century was characterised by a moral panic about prostitution and sexually transmitted diseases.[56] The prostitute destabilised the construction of sexual difference between men and women in that she represented the sexualised woman, the whore, in contradiction to the asexual ideal. Furthermore, she was not contained but crossed social boundaries in two ways. Firstly, in her overt sexuality, she disrupted the social construction of femininity itself. Secondly, she crossed a class boundary to potentially 'pollute' and infect the middle-class male. As Douglas says, '... physical crossing of the social barrier is treated as a dangerous pollution – the polluter becomes a doubly wicked object of reprobation, first because [she] crossed the line and second because [she] endangered others.'[57] As discussed previously, 'feeble-minded' women were increasingly being constructed in terms of immorality and fecundity. Conversely, women who were defined as immoral were increasingly likely to be labelled as 'feeble-minded'. At the beginning of the twentieth century, the Mental Deficiency Bill (1913) was criticised by Josiah Wedgwood, as it 'was one whereby prostitutes could be sent to feeble-minded houses to save mankind from infection ... this was a clear case of expediency vs. justice.'[58] As Mathew Thomson has commented, discourses of female sexuality were gradually changing towards the early part of the twentieth century, from constructing women as in need of protection from moral vice to constructing them as a potential threat to the body of the community.[59]

Conclusion

This leads full circle back to Mabel's story. As Mabel said, her mother had not committed any crime; her 'crime' was to be poor and to have given birth to a child outside marriage. This was sufficient for her to be labelled as 'feeble-minded' and 'immoral', to be seen as a threat rather than in need of support and help, and consequently to be segregated from the rest of society.

This chapter has charted a long path from the structure and ideas of the nineteenth century to one individual life story in the twentieth century. Crossing boundaries has been examined in a much more abstract way than physical lines of demarcation. However, classificatory systems and discourses are not separate from the world but have very real consequences and effects, as Mabel's story shows. One major consequence of the sets of ideas discussed was the Mental Deficiency Act of 1913, a critical piece of legislation and a framework for dealing with mental impairment for most of the twentieth century.[60] A woman could come under the umbrella of the Act for merely being destitute or in receipt of Poor Relief at the time of giving birth to an illegitimate child, or when pregnant with such a child. Mabel's mother was in this situation at a time when conceptual and physical boundaries were being tightly re-drawn; segregating her may or may not have been expedient, but it was certainly not just.

---

[12] Mental impairment is used here as a term that is relatively 'neutral'. Historically, as discourses defining mental impairment have shifted, so have the specific words used to label people; from idiots, imbeciles and feeble minded to subnormal and handicapped. Throughout I will either use the term impairment or the most historically appropriate term, even though the latter may reflect constructions that this work as a whole is challenging. It should be noted that within the self-advocacy movement, People First recommend the use of the term 'learning difficulties'.

[13] Discussed in M. Douglas, *Purity and Danger: An Analysis of the Concepts of Pollution and Taboo,* (London and New York: Routledge), 1966.

[14] Douglas, *Purity and Danger*, p.42.

[15] Discourse refers to a set of statements, ideas or meanings which have a specific history or, as Michel Foucault termed it, a genealogy. A discourse can therefore be seen as a set of rules which distinguishes it from other discourses and establishes the boundaries within which a phenomena can be made sense of and understood. It therefore defines its own truth and 'conditions of possibility'. In this sense, a discourse is 'knowledge' since 'knowledge'

is the power to set norms and to define what shall count as a 'fact'. See P. Abbott and R. Sapsford, 'The Body Politic, Health, Family and Society (Unit 11)', in *Social Problems and Social Welfare,* (Milton Keynes: The Open University Press, 1988), pp.61-65.

[16] For a more detailed discussion see J. Anderson, 'The United Kingdom: Legacies of the Past', in J. Anderson and M. Ricci, (eds.), *Society and Social Science: A Reader,* (Milton Keynes: The Open University, 1990), p.16.

[17] These statistics are provided by Lee, 1979 and discussed in D. Massey, 'A Global Sense of Place (unit 23)', *Society and Social Science: A Foundation Course,* (Milton Keynes: The Open University, 1991), p.29.

[18] Massey, 'A Global Sense of Place', p.32.

[19] See A. Oakley, *Housewife,* (Harmondsworth: Penguin, 1976).

[20] For example, the Mines Act in 1842 banned the employment of women as miners and from 1841 committees of male workers were calling for the exclusion of women from the factories. See M. Haralambos and M. Holborn, *Sociology: Themes and Perspectives (Third Edition),* (Hammersmith: Collins Educational, 1991), p.545.

[21] Massey, 'A Global Sense of Place', p.35.

[22] See Oakley, *Housewife.*

[23] This idea is expanded in J. Ryan, and R. Thomas, *The Politics of Mental Handicap,* (Harmondsworth, Middlesex, England; New York: Penguin Books, 1980), p.101.

[24] M. Oliver draws upon Finkelstein's work to develop this argument in M. Oliver, *The Politics of Disablement,* (Houndmills, Basingstoke, Hampshire, London: The Macmillan Press Ltd., 1990), p.27.

[25] Ryan and Thomas, *The Politics of Mental Handicap,* p.99.

[26] For further discussion see M. A. Crowther, *The Workhouse System 1834-1929: The History of an English Institution,* (London: Batsford Academic and Educational Ltd., 1981).

[27] See K. Jones, *A History of the Mental Health Services,* (London and Boston: Routledge and Kegan Paul, 1972), pp.183-4.

[28] For further discussion see Crowther, *The Workhouse System.*

[29] See Althusser cited in Oliver, *The Politics of Disablement,* p.32.

[30] The term eugenics is derived from the Greek, *eugenes,* which means good in stock or hereditarily endowed with noble qualities. The theory and practice of eugenics was to encourage fertility among those who were seen as favourably hereditarily endowed and discourage fertility among the lesser endowed to further the improvement of the 'race'.

[31] See F. Galton, *Inquiries into Human Faculty,* (London: Macmillan and Co., 1883), p.224.

[32] See R. Miles, 'Representations of the Other', in *Racism,* (London: Routledge, Chapman and Hall, 1989).

[33] Miles, *Racism.*

[34] Ryan and Thomas, *The Politics of Mental Handicap,* p.105.

[35] See D. Barker, 'How to Curb the Fertility of the Unfit: The Feeble Minded in Edwardian Britain', *Oxford Review of Education,* 9(3), (1983), 197-211.

[36] Douglas, *Purity and Danger,* p.vii.

[37] Douglas, *Purity and Danger,* p.123.

[38] Douglas, *Purity and Danger,* p.96.

[39] Cited in Jones, *A History of the Mental Health Services,* p.183.

[40] Discussed in Jones, *A History of the Mental Health Services,* p.182.

[41] E. Séguin, *Idiocy: And its Treatment by the Physiological Method* (Albany, New York: Brandow Printing Company, 1866), p.29.

[42] W. Wolfensberger, *The Principle of Normalisation in Human Services,* (Toronto: National Institute on Mental Retardation, 1972), p.16.

[43] Discussed in M. Rosen, G. R. Clark and M. S. Kivitz, *The History of Mental Retardation, Collected Papers, Vol.1,* (University Park Press, 1976).

[44] Cited in Crowther, *The Workhouse System,* p.257.

[45] F. Williams, 'Women with Learning Difficulties are Women too', in Langan, M. and Day, L. (eds), *Women, Oppression and Social Work: Issues in Anti-Discriminatory Practice,* (London: Unwin Hyam, 1992), p.150.

[46] C. Darwin, *The Origin of Species* (Sixth Edition), (London: John Murray, 1872).

[47] Williams, *Women, Oppression and Social Work.*

[48] Cited in Williams, *Women, Oppression and Social Work,* p.153.

[49] B. Ehrenreich and D. English, *For Her Own Good: 150 Years of the Experts' Advice to Women,* (London: Pluto Press, 1979), p.8.

[50] W. R. Greg, cited in M. Poovey, *Uneven Developments: The Ideological Work of Gender in Mid-Victorian England,* (London: Virago, 1988), p.2.

[51] Poovey, *Uneven Developments.*

[52] Poovey, *Uneven Developments,* p.10.

[53] Séguin, *Idiocy: And its Treatment by the Physiological Method,* p.59.

[54] Séguin cited in W. Ireland, *Idiocy and Imbecility,* (London: J. and A. Churchill, 1877), p.31.

[55] Séguin, *Idiocy: And its Treatment by the Physiological Method.*

[56] Poovey, *Uneven Developments,* p.30.

[57] M. Douglas cited in S. Delamont and L. Duffin, *The Nineteenth-Century Woman: The Cultural and Physical World,* (London: Croom Helm Ltd.; New York: Barnes and Noble Books, 1978), p.23.

[58] J. Wedgewood cited in Jones, *A History of the Mental Health Services,* p.201.

[59] M. Thomson, *The Problem of Mental Deficiency: Eugenics, Democracy and Social Policy in Britain c.1870-1959,* (Oxford: Clarendon Press, 1998).

[60] J. Walmsley, *Gender, Caring and Learning Disability,* (Unpublished PhD Thesis, The Open University, 1994), p.320.

Chapter 5

Concrete representations of a social category: consolidating and transforming public institutions for people classified as 'defective'

Patricia Potts

Summary

In this chapter Patricia Potts examines ways in which buildings designed for children and adults classified as 'defective' reflect the social status associated with that label. She also explores the possibility of adaptations that would give residents and users a more positive image and experience of life. She begins by illustrating medical and psychological systems of classifying people and goes on to discuss a range of public institutions, built between the 1850s and the 1990s. She argues that attempts to make sense of classifications of social categories have neglected their concrete manifestations, and that an architecture which could reflect more equitable social relations would have to challenge some fundamental assumptions.

Introduction

My chapter is based on two premises. The first is that considerations of the architecture, that is the concrete representations of social categories, have been neglected in attempts to make sense of these socially constructed categories. The second is that an architecture which can reflect equitable social relations has to challenge some fundamental assumptions.

From the mid-nineteenth century until the official abolition of categories of disability in 1981, the classification of human beings in terms of their assumed capacity to learn has aped the method of natural scientists. Just as living species were named and ranked according to their evolutionary supremacy, so strata of different kinds of learner were identified and fixed along a vertical scale. The attempt to construct a hermetic seal between 'normal' and 'subnormal' groups of people was led, in England, by medical practitioners, one of whose aims was to control the spread of social disease; a pathology in which 'degeneracy' became a dominant fear.[61]

In this human genealogy, physical and mental characteristics were believed to correspond closely, making visual imagery a central component of the process of identification. Because of this, critical discussion of the relationship between visual and verbal languages of social classification has focused on the proposed types of people. However, there are other non-verbal dimensions that may be just as relevant to the understanding of social hierarchies. The human status of different people was, and is, reflected in the topography of public institutions, and the visual language of built environments is thus a rich source of meanings. In asking why barriers were erected between groups of people and what are the possibilities of breaking them down, it does not make sense to ignore the effects of organised space.[62]

A number of factors came together to promote the building of institutions for separated categories of people: the cost of providing for unemployed, sick and destitute people before the introduction of the Welfare State; the influence of medicine as an emerging profession; the particular difficulties experienced by working-class people in the expanding industrial cities; the distinction between criminals and paupers, lunatics and idiots, both from those who argued that this would facilitate more humane provision and from those who saw the task as one of social control; and the development of psychometric testing. I cannot discuss these issues in detail here but they form the background to the proliferation of specialised public institutions in England over the last hundred and fifty years.[63] (See Chapter 4 for a more extensive discussion.)

Differentiation between groups of people in the nineteenth century seemed to represent social progress in line with developments in science. Architecture was bound to respond. Order is a fundamental concept in architecture, as in society, associated with stability, intelligibility, safety and survival. However, despite the exposure, in the 1970s, of the damaging consequences of social classification systems and subsequent campaigns for their dissolution, the distinctions persist in official documentation as well as in common speech. It is not surprising that specialised problem-solving dominates over flexibility and diversity when it comes to designing buildings for supposedly homogeneous groups.

I begin by looking at some influential expressions of a system of social classification. Then I discuss examples of design for people identified as having physical or mental difficulties, sufficient to justify segregation into asylums, hospitals and special schools. I go on to discuss how far buildings can be transformed in response to changing value-systems. Finally, I draw out the implications of these discussions for an architecture that could reflect the crossing of social boundaries rather than the shoring-up of social pathology.

Classifying social and intellectual competence

In this section, I examine three approaches to classification, derived from beliefs about racial stereotypes, disease and intelligence. A fourth example illustrates how they were translated into advice about the design of public institutions.

My first example of a classification system is that developed by Dr John Langdon-Down. He famously used an analogy with race in his classification of socially incompetent people:

> *I had for some time had my attention directed to the*
> *possibility of making a classification of the feeble-minded,*
> *by arranging them around various ethnic standards ... A*
> *very large number of congenital idiots are typical Mongols.*

> *So marked is this it is difficult to realize that they are the
> children of Europeans; but so frequently are these
> characteristics presented, that there can be no doubt that
> these ethnic features are the result of degeneration.*[64]

The stereotype was fleshed out:

> *Mongols are usually placid and happy idiots whose bodies
> bear ample evidence of the widespread constitutional
> nature of the abnormality ... Idiots are wholly dependent.
> They cannot be taught to feed themselves, or to keep
> themselves clean, nor can they recognize other people or
> communicate with them except in the crudest and most
> primitive way. They are in fact considerably less
> intelligent than domestic animals.*[65]

This does not come from another of Langdon-Down's own lectures at
the London Hospital or from the writings of an immediate follower. It
was written by Dr David Stafford-Clark in 1950. His book *Psychiatry
Today* was reprinted regularly for more than twenty years and was
a core textbook for medical and paramedical professionals. The
rigidity and resilience of this kind of social typology is illustrated by
the story of a young man who had been excluded from school as
ineducable and who lived at home with his mother. He ran errands
and, after his mother's heart attack (this was at the very time
Stafford-Clark was reinforcing our belief in his incompetence),
took responsibility for all domestic chores and administration. He
was literate and could play the piano. Social workers noted that his
mother could not continue to live at home without his help.
However, when his mother died, he was sent to a residential
institution.[66]

By the turn of the twentieth century, the language of classification
had become more pathological. My second example is taken from
Mental Deficiency by Dr A. F. Tredgold,[67] first published in 1908
(see Table 1). It remained a textbook well into the twentieth century
and was reprinted many times. It was illustrated with mass-
reproduced portrait photographs. You will see that the identification
of 'amentia' was assumed to be both complex and unproblematic,
a set of pathological human variations whose 'discovery' was made
possible by advances in medical science.

Table 1 - CLASSIFICATION OF AMENTIA

	Etiology	Pathology	Clinical Varieties (These may be any of the Three Degrees - Idiocy, Imbecility, and Feeble-mindedness.)
PRIMARY AMENTIA — PATHOLOGICAL GERMINAL VARIATIONS	due to { Ancestral alcoholism, tuberculosis, syphilis, and other causes, and manifested by presence in family of amentia, insanity, epilepsy, etc.	A numerical deficiency, irregular arrangement and imperfect development of cortical neurones.	1. SIMPLE. 2. MICROCEPHALIC. 3. MONGOLIAN.
SECONDARY AMENTIA — I. GROSS CEREBRAL LESIONS	1) *Toxic–viz.,* pneumonia, scarlet fever, influenza, measles, syphilis, smallpox, enteric, encephalitis, meningitis, etc. 2) *Mechanical–viz.,* haemorrhage, embolism, thrombosis, trauma.	An arrested development of cortical neurones corresponding to site of lesion. Final results are - Localized atrophy, softening, cysts, sclerosis, pseudoporencephaly and hemiatrophy.	4. SYPHILITIC. 5. AMAUROTIC. 6. HYDROCEPHALIC. 7. PORENCEPHALIC. 8. SCLEROTIC. 9. PARALYTIC 10. *Other* TOXIC, INFLAMMATORY *and* VASCULAR.
II. DEFECTIVE CEREBRAL NUTRITION	due to { 1) *Via* BLOOD: Qualitative and quantitative defects due to specific glandular inadequacy, etc. 2) *Via* NEURONES: Isolation or disease of special sense organs leading to defective stimuli from without.	General arrest of neuronic development.	11. EPILEPTIC. 12. CRETINISM. 13. NUTRITIONAL.
		Localized arrest of neuronic development.	14. ISOLATION.

Reprinted from: *Mental Deficiency*, Tredgold A. F. (1908) by permission of the publisher Baillière Tindall

Dr Tredgold was Medical Expert to the Royal Commission on the Care and Control of the Feeble-Minded (1904-8), whose Report was eventually followed by legislation for the compulsory detention of those identified in institutions administered by a new Board of Control, which, for these purposes, replaced the Local Government Board, the Lunacy Commission and the Home Office. At a meeting at the House of Commons in 1911 to introduce the Bill, Tredgold said:

> *With regard to their intellect, human beings are divisible*
> *into two great groups – the normal and the defective.*
> *The normal group consists of individuals of very varying*
> *capacity, ranging from extreme brilliance to dullness. The*
> *defective group likewise consists of persons of very varying*
> *intelligence, but for convenience it is divided into three*
> *degrees, namely,* idiocy, imbecility *and* feeble-mindedness
> *[Dr Tredgold's emphases].*[68]

This speech was printed in an appendix to an issue of the Eugenics Review to which Dr Tredgold contributed an article on 'The Future Progress of Man', in which he made it clear that the 'normal' and 'defective' corresponded to the 'fit' (a 'progressive' human variation) and 'unfit' (a 'retrogressive' variation):

> *Such, then, are the two chief forms of variation. It is*
> *obvious that those of the first kind – the fit – are essential*
> *to progress; that if the race is to develop it must give rise to*
> *individuals who can do more than mark time, who can*
> *advance. On the other hand it is equally obvious that the*
> *pathological variations – the unfit – are inimical to progress.*
> *They are incapable of advance, they are falling by the way*
> *in the march of civilisation. They may actually impede a*
> *nation's advance by withdrawing for their support the*
> *energy and resources of the more capable members of the*
> *community. There can be little doubt that the future of any*
> *society will be dependent upon the relative preponderance*
> *of these two variations.*[69]

My third example is taken from *The Fundamentals of School Health* by Dr James Kerr,[70] published in 1926 (see Table 2). Unlike Tredgold's chart, it outlines a full range of human capacity.

Dividing lines between the groups are sharpened by the use of numerical Intelligence Quotients, reflecting the growing influence of psychology in the assessment of learning capacities. The language of 'low-grades' and 'high-grades' was still common when I was teaching in special schools in the 1970s and IQ testing remained a mainstay of educational psychologists for years afterwards.[71]

Table 2 - CLASSIFICATION OF INTELLIGENCE

Low-grade amentia:	Idiots	Approximate I.Q.	– 25
	Imbeciles	Ineducable	25 – 50
High-grade amentia:	Mentally defective	Morons	50 – 70
		Border-line	70 – 80
Normal:		Dull	80 – 90
		Average	90 – 110
		Good	110 – 120
Super-normal:		Excellent	120 – 140
		Super-excellent	140 –

From: Kerr, J. (1926) *The Fundamentals of School Health*, London, George Allen & Unwin Ltd.
Chapter XXI: 'Subnormal Intelligence'
Table taken from Classification made by Terman, using his revised Stanford scale.

Dr Kerr was Consulting Medical Officer to the London County Council at the time of writing his book. There is a long chapter on 'Subnormal Intelligence', with descriptions of a range of specific types. There is also a chapter on 'Sites and Buildings', in which the role of the medical officer is presented as important as the architect and the education officer, because of the manifest health problems caused by poor ventilation, sanitation, heating and lighting, and by cramped spaces which prevented exercise and encouraged contagious disease. Before he came to London, Dr Kerr had worked in Bradford and Birmingham. His description of visiting elementary schools in London shows that he accepted that physical environments conveyed a social and psychological meaning:

The writer's first impression of London schools was the poverty-stricken, mean appearance of even a well-furnished school-room given by the bare bricks of the wall, painted or washed over without cement. The psychological effect of such a room is very harmful according to modern ideas, producing the sense of inferiority.[72]

When it came to the 'defective', however, these sensitivities disappeared, as if there were an unbridgeable gap, in his mind, between 'normal' and 'abnormal' groups:

It is in the realm of the socially defective that heredity becomes of overwhelming practical importance. The next move in the regulation of human affairs is not legislation to promote eugenics, but legislation to cut off the threads of defective human descent. This means segregation or sterilisation of carriers of degeneracy. At present, economic laws are tending to destroy the threads of superior kind. Little is being done to remedy the evil.[73]

My last example comes from the Board of Control. Although the Mental Deficiency Act of 1913 remained the central framework for services provided by the Board, the terms of the Local Government Act of 1929 introduced a significant development, as it transferred to County and County Borough Councils all property that had belonged to the Poor Law Authorities, now abolished. There is detailed advice on the size of 'colonies' and the classification of inmates:

To secure efficiency, proper classification and economy, a Colony for mental defectives should provide for not less than from 400 to 500 cases. The best size, from the point of view of administration, is from 1,000 to 1,200, but the Board would see no objection to a maximum approximating to 2,000...

Adequate facilities are essential for the classification of mental defectives. Under this term are included idiots, imbeciles and feeble-minded, and these classes vary widely in the requirements of their daily life and cannot be associated together without detriment to the happiness of each class. Methods of training and of recreation should also be varied according to the different grades and ages, and can only be successfully carried out by grouping together defectives of the same mentality. Proper classification tends to lighten the arduous duties of teachers and nurses, and its value is recognised by parents when visiting their children.

Active children and adults should be sub-divided and classified according to their age and mental characteristics. If the classification of each group is to be satisfactory the higher grade, the medium grade and the lower grade should be separated from one another, and there should be some age classification within the adult groups. The classification will also be complicated by the presence of epileptics and patients of defective or objectional habits. The greater the sub-division, the better for the happiness of the patients, and the greater the number to be dealt with in each group, the easier it is to arrange buildings for each group. It will, therefore, be seen that when the numbers are limited, the classification must suffer.[74]

Buildings for 'idiots'

The asylum for idiots at Earlswood Common, Redhill, Surrey was the first institution in England to provide exclusively for people identified as 'idiots'. Previously, they would been have been admitted to workhouses, prisons or lunatic asylums. An engraving of the asylum was published in 1854 as part of a campaign to raise funds for its completion. The accompanying text tells us that:

The main object in the design of the edifice (after considering the convenience of arrangement and classification) is to present to the eye of the unfortunate inmates nothing that is not calculated to produce an agreeable impression. The apartments will therefore throughout be finished in a neat and pleasing, but at the same time, economic, style. Provision is, however, made for a few superior cases, or inmates, whose friends are willing to pay for the great advantages, in point of treatment, obtainable in an institution of this description.[75]

You can see in Figure 3 that the asylum resembles a palatial country house. The people walking in the grounds create an atmosphere of gentility. There are no high walls. Fresh air and the opportunity for physical exercise were listed as particular benefits. The sponsors described the project as a 'work of mercy'.

Figure 3 - Asylum, Earlswood

A decade later, Earlswood was described in similar tones:

> *Nothing surprises a visitor to a well-managed asylum for imbeciles than the entire absence of that gloom which most persons naturally expect to find hanging over it like a dark cloud ... Even the feeblest seem calm and contented.*[76]

However, when John Langdon-Down went to Earlswood in 1858 as Superintendant Physician, at the age of thirty, he found something rather different:

> *Earlswood was in disorder. It was owned by a private charity which in 1855 had transferred all its patients from Park House, Highgate to new and only half built premises in Surrey. The move was made with what looks like unreasonable haste and certainly without the required*

statutory notice to the Commissioners in Lunacy.
Successive reports by visiting Commissioners
described appalling conditions ... Nine months after
opening it was still without a properly surfaced
carriage approach, the water supply was inadequate
and sewage was discharged into open pits.[77]

While living conditions remained poor at Earlswood, Langdon-Down nevertheless built up a reputation for enlightened treatment, along the lines of what we would now call 'life skills'. A year after the Commissioners reported continuing problems with diet, health and safety, the British Medical Journal applauded an alternative story:

Forethought, ingenuity, kindness and benevolence have
triumphed over the most distressing deficiency of intellect
and inferiority of organisation. Order and cleanliness
reign every where, the faintest gleams of intelligence
are encouraged and the slightest capabilities utilised.[78]

So while it can be argued that Earlswood represented just another kind of prison, with an exterior attractive to subscribers, visitors and the local population, it can also be seen as an indication of the contemporary belief that this new kind of work with 'idiots' would yield positive results, that they could and should be educated:

The benefits to be derived from the establishment of a
school for this class of persons, upon humane and
scientific principles, would be very great. Not only would
all idiots who should be received into it be improved in
their bodily and mental condition ... it would be
demonstrated that no idiot need be confined or restrained
by force ... and there is not one of any age who may not be
made more of a man and less of a brute by patience and
kindness directed by energy and skill.[79]

Now look at the geography of St Lawrence's, also in Surrey, which opened as an idiot asylum in 1870. Thirteen four-storey T-shaped blocks regimented on the two wings of an encampment of administrative buildings, workshops and other facilities. There is no escaping its penitential character. Earlswood was built for around four hundred residents. St Lawrence's housed well over a thousand. It was a world apart and accommodated a shift in political and professional attitudes away from 'alleviation' towards compulsory detention and sterilisation.

Figure 4 - St Lawrence's, Caterham, Surrey

Mabel Cooper went to St Lawrence's in 1952 at the age of seven (see Chapter 3). By then it would have been called a 'subnormality' hospital or a hospital for 'mentally handicapped' people. Mabel lived there for over twenty years. She did not experience anything called 'education' but she remembers making baskets. Since leaving for a new life in the community, Mabel has written her autobiography:

> *When I first went in there, even just getting out of the car you could hear the racket. You think you're going to a madhouse. When you first went there you could hear people screaming and shouting outside. It was very noisy but I think you do get used to them after a little while because it's like everywhere that's big. If there's lots of people you get lots of noise, and they had like big dormitories, didn't they. And the children were just as noisy, in the children's home, and they were all the same sort of people ...*
>
> *There was bars on the windows when I first went to St Lawrence's, it was just like a prison. Of course it was called a nuthouse in them days, so it used to have bars on it.*

*You couldn't open the windows. Well, you could, but not
far enough to get out of them. You didn't have toys, no
toys whatsoever. You couldn't have toys because they
would just get broken and thrown through the bars in the
window, and get caught in them ...*

*It was big. There were lots and lots of wards. On the
female side it was A to H. On the male side it was A to D.
They all had about 75 people in. And then there was little
houses on the grounds and they had about 50 people in ...*

*The ward was blocked off, there was doors. You weren't allowed
to sit on your beds. The beds were that close to one another, so
you couldn't have anything private ...*[81]

By 1981 Mabel had left St Lawrence's Hospital. This was the
International Year of Disabled People. That year, publicity in news-
papers and on television contributed to the beginning of the end for the
long-stay hospitals. St Lawrence's has now been demolished, its identity
as a ghetto for stigmatised people too strong for any transformation.
Earlswood, meanwhile, is being converted into luxury flats.

Purpose-building

Look at Figure 5. What function could this building have?

Figure 5

Notes which accompany the publication of this design provide some clues:

> *The use of a heavy structure is reinforced by small windows facing North whilst the South facing elements are opened over a treed garden. The usually open nature of primary schools is not possible here due to the technical needs of enclosure: children are normally taught at special desks set out in a horse shoe arrangement and the octagon is the nearest and most economical shape for containment ...*
>
> *To preserve internal quietude the building presents an unyielding protective wall to the main roads – the traffic noise source. Air-conditioning is necessary as the school is sealed from the outside: in the centre is the cooling tower above a plant room.*[82]

These outside walls remind me of wartime pill-boxes on a remote East Anglian coast. In fact, this is Frank Barnes School, a school for primary-aged deaf children. There are three special schools on the same site in North London, two built in the 1960s and this one between 1973 and 1978. The aim of the whole project was to provide an acoustically perfect environment for 80 deaf children. As a result, despite the increased window space along the inner walls facing the garden (see Figure 6a), it appears to the local community as a series of padded cells, in which there is no place for hearing people or any other noisy distractions.

Figure 6a

Figure 6b. Frank Barnes School - teaching cell

Figure 6b illustrates one of these teaching cells, with its minute single window, blind drawn. The architectural notes continue to stress the 'otherness' of the pupils:

> *A typical classroom, octagonal in plan to contain eight desks. This polygonal form also helps to break up confusing echoes and diffuse sound giving the quietest background possible for the teaching of deaf children. The floor and the ceiling contain induction loops to reinforce amplified sound to individual hearing aids.*[83]

It is clear that the pedagogy of the school is based on an oral/aural approach, not on British Sign Language, although this might be assumed to be the first language of deaf children. Briefings with teaching staff and the education authority did not seem to involve any discussion of these highly contentious issues. The deaf community has put forward compelling arguments for separate provision, but based on their identity as members of a particular (but largely rejected) culture, in which, like any other cultural community, language is central. A special school which separates children and yet is focused on their assimilation into a 'normality' which remains beyond the sound barrier of the school, seems bound to fail to secure the pupils' active membership of either kind of community.

In contrast to the fortifications of Frank Barnes School, there is a new special school in North East London built of cosy red brick; it could be a Tesco store on the edge of town.

Figure 7 - Waverley School, North East London

Waverley School opened in 1992, and its pupils are children and young people identified as having 'severe learning difficulties'. The introduction to an article about the school tells us that:

> ... to cater for users with severe learning and physical disabilities, normal design rules had to be thrown out of the window. The result is a beautifully thought-out school that stimulates and motivates.[84]

The school, then housed in an old three-storey building, had originally opened in 1971 when responsibility for children previously seen as 'ineducable' and now reclassified as 'Educationally Subnormal (Severe)' was transferred from the Department of Health to the Department of Education and Science. In 1985, Her Majesty's Inspectors condemned the accommodation and plans were made for the new school, whose aims and approach are outlined in the following way by the head teacher:

> The ultimate aim of the school is that each child shall maximise their potential and therefore achieve as great a sense of independence as possible.

All pupils at Waverley have full access to their environment and learning experiences are delivered in motivating, challenging and age-appropriate situations ...

The excellent facilities at Waverley provide many opportunities for exciting curricular activities, creating a busy atmosphere and offering stimulation and challenge. This in turn helps the child to achieve, thereby gaining confidence, self-esteem and a sense of worth. Emphasis is always placed on the individual child.[85]

An article in the Architects' Journal described the translation of this ethos into design solutions:

The school, which is really four schools in one, can accommodate 120 pupils in departments for nursery/reception, infants/junior, seniors and 16+. The 16+ department takes the form of a separate unit, linked to the main school by a porte-cochère and positioned to relate to Enfield College on the neighbouring site, where it is intended that some pupils will progress to further education.

The three departments forming the main school have been condensed around an indoor swimming pool and a central courtyard garden. This gives an unusually large (4000m²) single-storey building, under pitched roofs, with a very low wall-to-floor ratio. This in turn offers the scope for a high level of energy efficiency, a factor of key importance given the very costly nature of running a special school wih high staffing ratios and exceptional space demands ...

Although the new school is a large building, its bulk has been broken up and it certainly does not feel intimidating ... Nearly all corridors allow ventilation and light to classrooms through roof windows ... The significance of the floor as a resource for the children has been particularly well appreciated, and they can enjoy looking out when spending time sitting or lying at floor level ... Tiled murals in the pool areas are derived from the children's drawings and the whole atmosphere is of fun and enjoyment.[86]

The exterior is domestic, accessible, not forbidding or impenetrable like Frank Barnes School. There is light and colour and space. I visited the school with the head teacher of a mainstream school. The impression I had was of peace, quiet, emptiness. None of the noise and chaos I remembered from the sister schools I had taught in. The atmosphere was not 'busy' and I did not feel the energy of 'challenge', 'stimulation', 'excitement' and 'confidence'. The inner courtyard had a rock garden and Bonsai trees and was restful in a clinical sort of way.

My colleague was expecting that, as a result of his visit, he would at last agree to the transfer of one of his students. He had become concerned that his school was not meeting her needs as well as he had hoped. However, instead of being convinced that the special school was the right place for her, he came away disturbed by what we had seen. One of the arguments for segregating this teenager was that her social life would be better in the special school. We saw that the chances of peer-group friendship for the students could not be great with a total of 25 students in the four departments, each one divided into three classes.

What really struck my colleague was the distribution of resources. More than five million pounds had been spent on around 120 pupils. While accepting that the students in the school do require additional equipment and facilities, it still seemed an enormous sum of money to spend on segregating such a small number of children; especially when the policy of the local authority was to provide increased support in the ordinary schools. What sort of support systems could have been set up in mainstream schools with five million pounds?

Waverley's wonderful facilities appeared under-used and, coming from a school where the students often had to make do with over-crowding and inadequate resources, this was provocative to my companion. We experienced what seemed to be the total opposite of the conditions I have described as characterising Victorian institutions and we wondered how to make sense of it. It is clear that the pressure to segregate is as strong today as it was then. The precision of imaginative modern design solutions attests to the enduring belief in discrete categories of human being. Decisions about matching facilities to educational requirements seem to have ignored the social and political consequences of specialisation, or else these consequences are not seen as all that important for the students at schools like Waverley or Frank Barnes. Yet the rhetoric of their providers is one of independence and an ordinary life. Surely the design issue is how to incorporate into the diversity of mainstream services the particular requirements of all students? The social costs of hi-tech isolation seem to me to be too high.

Purpose-building usually reflects an exceptionally high or an exceptionally low status of user or function: special school; opera house. 'We' do not talk about purpose-built homes or comprehensive schools because they are for a heterogeneous 'us'. Purpose-building refers to the separation of a specialised function, prepared for 'them'.

Transformations

Can the identity and purpose of specialised buildings be adapted to reflect changing social and political attitudes? Here is the story of an attempt at the transformation of an institution which had begun as a 'Colony for mental defectives'. My information comes from a history being written by a retired Medical Director and from personal correspondence with the Principal Nursing Officer who was in post during the 1970s and 1980s.

St Andrew's Colony in Morpeth, Northumberland, was opened in 1938, with five villas completed. The plan was for 1,000 residents, a number never achieved. At the opening ceremony, Alderman McHugh was keen to stress that, 'This is not a mental hospital but a colony for the mentally defective. There is a great difference between the two.' In its first year, the Commissioners of the Board of Control noted that the 113 men and 103 women were, 'mostly of a high-grade class and among them some of delinquent type who had already given some cause for anxiety.'

During the 1940s, St Andrews quickly became overcrowded, with 75 people in villas designed for 60. In 1947 a major expansion was planned: five 'low grade' blocks with 40 places each, two adult blocks of 60 places each, a children's block with 50 places and eight new staff cottages. One hundred acres of additional land was acquired, to provide for 400 people in the short term, with an ultimate maximum of 1,400, reflecting the Board of Control's thinking about the benefits of size. In 1948, however, the National Health Service took over the running of the Colony, which then became known as the Northgate and District Hospital. In 1950 there were over 600 residents. Developments included Occupational Therapy, workshops and a unit for 'difficult patients of all grades'.

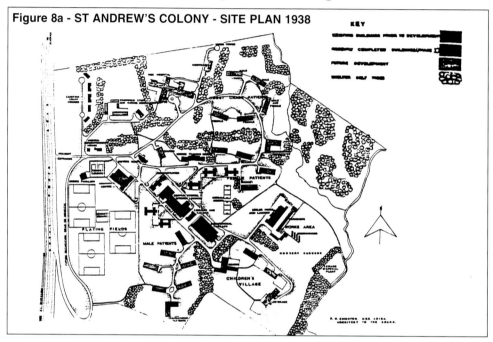

Figure 8a - ST ANDREW'S COLONY - SITE PLAN 1938

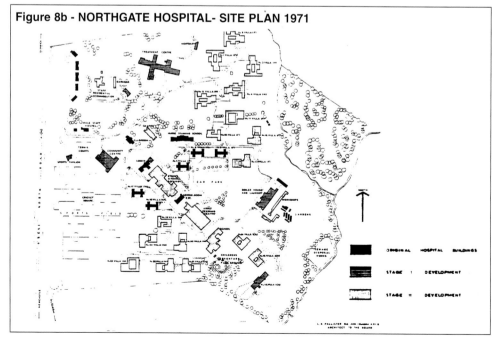

Figure 8b - NORTHGATE HOSPITAL- SITE PLAN 1971

In 1965 a range of recreational and therapeutic facilities were built but no adult villas, despite the overcrowding. When the new facilities were opened, the Minister of Health, Kenneth Robinson, referred to changes in public attitudes and the possibilities of care in the community. However, a second phase of developments went ahead and was completed in 1971: six female villas, nine male villas, a school, an adult training centre, a new dining hall and kitchen and a nurses' home.

> *These developments reflected the self-contained institutional care philosophy prevailing at the time of planning although the treatment centre concept was more far-sighted ... By the time building began thinking had changed ... but it proved impossible to achieve more than minuscule changes under pain of having to go back to the drawing board.*[89]

The Principal Nursing Officer set out to create the atmosphere of ordinary life for the residents:

> *My own view is that the place where people live not only determines the attitudes of staff but the public at large. I thought that by furnishing the new villas at Northgate in the early 1970s with domestic furniture, i.e. divans, carpets, wallpaper, normal living-room furniture etc. and integrating men and women, that a very normal lifestyle would be provided for mentally handicapped people.*[90]

It was impossible:

> *Nurse training was not geared to this style of living and even if it was, they were not in the practical situation fulfilling the total role of home-maker. Domestics were employed in villas to do domestic work – the meals were cooked in a central kitchen and laundry was washed in a central laundry. The person in charge of the villa does not have a budget so all supplies are obtained centrally. The sitting and dining rooms were large to accommodate 30 people and because of the numbers that had to be accommodated the architecture of the building did not resemble an ordinary house in any shape or form. The greatest drawback of course was that it was not in the middle of things but separated from society. Even if a villa was placed in the middle of society it would look extremely odd because of its size and difference from other buildings and of course this happens with purpose-built social services hostels.*[91]

The residents were going to have to leave the hospital altogether if they were to experience another kind of life. Children were the first to leave, five of them going to live in a council house in a nearby town in 1981. Notes written by the Core Home Leader six months later include descriptions of the changes in the children, whose real names are not used here:

> *Several people found it worrying to handle a child so profoundly mentally and physically handicapped, but in a short space of time everyone gained confidence. There has been a drastic decrease in David's vomiting and a definite increase in giggling and babbling noises ...*

> *For several weeks we were being woken by crying. However, this has stopped and we have discontinued night sedation. If we sit on the floor playing dominoes or cards Jane will scuffle over to us and try and put the pieces ...*

> *As the staff had seen his repertoire of eye poking, foot stamping, spitting and terrible behaviour at mealtimes, we were all prepared for the worst. However, the most difficult problem ... was probably his sleeping pattern, or more appropriately, his lack of one. Nick could manage quite nicely on $4\frac{1}{2}$ or $5\frac{1}{2}$ hours, but unfortunately we couldn't. Again night sedation was discontinued as ineffective. Now he usually sleeps from 10.45 p.m. until 7.00 a.m ... the headbanging which we observed shortly before leaving Northgate was found to be due to an ear infection, but when really tired or upset he will resort to this ...*

> *Of all the activities the children enjoy, I think one of the nicest ones to see is when Charlie, a normal boy living in the same street, comes and plays football with Mary and Nick.*

> *It is good to sit watching TV with the children and not worry about putting the laundry away.*

> *If it is a sunny day, we pack a picnic and go out and don't have to plan a week in advance.*[92]

Specialised institutions, detached from the diversity of ordinary life, do not seem to be capable of transformation in such a way as to enhance the social value of the residents for whom they were originally built.

Discussion

The huge size and isolation of the nineteenth century institutions for 'mentally defective' people helped to consolidate the social classification of thousands of supposedly similar people, who had not chosen segregation for themselves. A hundred years or so later, the project of classification and compulsory segregation is still going strong in educational contexts, with architects producing creative and technically advanced work in response. It is as if the high quality of these late twentieth-century buildings can somehow camouflage or trivialise the fact of exclusion.

If there are more than a thousand people in a self-sufficient institution, then there is obviously going to be an issue of control, especially if the physical and social environments are impoverished. If you have a tiny group of children and are going to spend a fortune on a school just for them, what does this mean? Does it really reflect a reversal of values? It may appear progressive, in that meeting the requirements of these students may cost more than for others, but in terms of involuntary segregation, what has changed? It does not seem to me that a brand new special school breaks down any barriers. Buildings which facilitate more democratic social relations than are possible with the rigidity of specialised forms require an architecture that can tolerate disorder. For there is no such thing as a 'class' of human beings, sharing a predetermined identity and set of interests. The challenge for designers, builders and users is to create environments which are mobile enough to respond to the dynamics of social and political change.

Acknowledgements

I should like to thank Lucy O'Leary, Corporate Policy Manager, Northgate and Prudhoe NHS Trust; Stuart Watson of the Builder Group; Charlotte Wood, Photographer, Marlborough, Wiltshire; and Dianne Bennell, Local Studies Library, Chesterfield.

[61] For further discussion which relates concerns about 'degeneracy' to ideas of 'pollution', see Lindsay Brigham (chapter 4).

[62] See Rob Kitchen, '"Out of Place", "Knowing One's Place": space, power and the exclusion of disabled people', *Disability and Society*, 13 (3), (1998), 343-356.

[63] See Andy Scull, *Decarceration*, (Princeton: Prentice-Hall, 1977) and C. Philo, '"Fit localities for an asylum": the historical geography of the "mad-business" in England viewed through the pages of the Asylum Journal', *Journal of Historical Geography*, 13, (1987), 398-415.

[64] J. Langdon-Down, 'Ethnic Classification of Idiots', *Clinical Lecture Reports*, 3, (London Hospital, 1866).

[65] D. Stafford-Clark, *Psychiatry Today* (1973 edition), (Harmondsworth: Penguin, 1950).

[66] See E. C. Butterfield, 'A provocative case of overachievement in a mongol', *American Journal of Mental Deficiency*, (1961), 444-448.

[67] A. F. Tredgold, *Mental Deficiency*, (London: Balliere, Tindall and Cox, 1908).

[68] A. F. Tredgold, 'Eugenics and the Future Progress of Man', *Eugenics Review*, 3, (April 1911-Jan 1912), see Appendix.

[69] Tredgold, *Eugenics Review*, 3, (April 1911-Jan 1912), p.97.

[70] J.Kerr, *The Fundamentals of School Health*, (London: George Allen and Unwin Ltd., 1926).

[71] Joanna Ryan (1972) 'I.Q. – The Illusion of Objectivity', in (eds) Richardson, K. and Spears, S. *Race, Culture and Intelligence*, Harmondsworth, Penguin.

[72] Kerr, Ibid., p.746.

[73] Kerr, *The Fundamentals of School Health*, p.94.

[74] *Board of Control*, 'Suggestions And Instructions Relating To The Arrangement And Construction Of Colonies For Defectives', (London, Board of Control, 1936), p.5.

[75] Print of Earlswood Idiot Asylum, *Illustrated London News*, 11th March, 1854, reproduced in Potts, P. (1982) *The Professionals*, Unit 7 of Open University Course 'Special Needs in Education' (E241) pp.20-1, Milton Keynes, Open University Press.

[76] See 'Idiot Asylums' (editorial), *Edinburgh Review*, 122 (249), (1865), 37-74.

[77] J. Earl, *Dr. Langdon-Down and the Normansfield Theatre*, (Borough of Twickenham Local History Society, 1997).

[78] *British Medical Journal*, 22 June, 1867 quoted in Earl, J. (1997) *Dr Langdon-Down and the Normansfield Theatre*, Twickenham, Borough of Twickenham Local History Society, occasional paper 6, p.8.

[79] Massachusetts House of Representatives (1848), quoted in L. Kanner, *A History of the Care and Study of the Mentally Retarded*, (USA, Charles Thomas, 1964), pp.41-2.

[80] See Patricia Potts, 'Origins', Unit 9 of Open University course, *Special Needs in Education*, (Milton Keynes: Open University Press, 1982) and Patricia Potts, 'Medicine, Morals and Mental Deficiency', *Oxford Review of Education*, 9 (3), (1983), 181-196.

[81] M. Cooper, 'Mabel Cooper's Life Story', in Atkinson, D., Jackson, M. and Walmsley, J. (eds), *Forgotten Lives. Exploring the History of Learning Disability*, (Kidderminster: BILD Publications, 1997), pp.22-23 and p.26.

[82] R. Ringshall, M. Miles and F. Kelsall, *The Urban School. Buildings for Education in London* 1870-1980, (London: Greater London Council and The Architectural Press, 1983), p.221.

[83] Ringshall and Kelsall, *The Urban School*, p.222.

[84] From article about the School: 5.6.92, p.3.

[85] Ibid., p.48.

[86] J. Penton, 'Meeting special needs. Waverley School, Enfield, and the Red Cross Centre, Irvine', *Architects' Journal*, (9 September, 1992), pp.24-29 and p.37.

[87] This quotation is taken from an unpublished history of Northgate, (1999).

[88] Ibid.

[89] Ibid.

[90] Extract from personal correspondence, 1982.

[91] Ibid.

[92] From notes written by Core Home Leader.

Chapter 6

Surprise journeys and border crossings

Sheena Rolph

Summary

In this chapter, Sheena Rolph tells the life history of Alice Chapman, using many different sources to explore her life and to illustrate aspects of the history of learning difficulties. Oral history and archives are combined to explore the reasons why Alice was able to move through many border crossings so that she eventually lived a more independent life, whereas for many this progression was not possible. Such an approach, that includes several voices, can be used to reconstruct life stories which would otherwise be lost, and to enrich our knowledge of the history of learning disability in the first half of the twentieth century. Comparisons are drawn with other women who were less successful than Alice in achieving an ordinary life.

Introduction

In my exploration of ways in which biographies and autobiographies can contribute to a history of community care (in Norfolk) in the twentieth century, two life-stories in particular have stood out, those of Alice Chapman and Marion Green. In the course of our talks, Marion Green offered to tell my fortune. She said, 'You will have a long life with surprise journeys.' This was a clear echo of her own life, and summed up in a telling phrase the experiences of many of those said to have learning difficulties who were detained under the Mental Deficiency Act in the first decades of the century. To understand and interpret these 'surprise journeys', I used the idea of examining the many border crossings in people's lives between ordinary life, institutions, and community care: why they took place; what happened at these crossings; the nature of the border controls; and what say the women themselves had in the decisions. Borders contain both tensions and links between one side and the other. They can become 'charged and energised' during moral panics, when they are clear and obvious; at other times they are hidden, invisible or blurred.[93] Another way of understanding the border crossings was to think of them in terms of inclusion or exclusion and the degrees to which people were able to take part in ordinary life. New writing by people with learning difficulties themselves argues against the 'victim' status so often given to them. In the everyday lives of the people I have been talking to there were ways of rebelling, asserting, mocking, and above all, surviving.

In this chapter, I discuss Alice's life story, referring also at various points to episodes in Marion's life that were either parallel or divergent, highlighting the importance of multiple voices, and the fact that, as Jan Walmsley has suggested, 'there is no one typical career of people with learning difficulties.'[94] By comparing the lives of Alice and Marion, I hope to throw some light on the variety of experiences, and the reasons why some women were able to negotiate the crossing of all the borders, whereas others remained within the control of the institution most of their lives.

Alice Chapman's Biography[95]

Constructing the biography

Some of the liveliest debates now taking place are between those who claim the history of learning disability as their own, maintaining

70

that there is no place within it for either authors or witnesses without a disability, and those, on the other hand, who are ready to include the views of others in order to construct a 'whole history'. (See Introduction and Chapter 1). In the reconstruction of Alice's life, the story-telling had several layers, and different voices. Alice died in 1969, but her friend and employer for 25 years, Mrs Pearce, has been telling me Alice's life story, both as Alice told it to her, and as Alice lived it with her. There are therefore three voices running through this account: Mrs Pearce's voice, because her own story begins to interweave with Alice's and because this is her history too; my own voice as the researcher; and Alice's voice, both when it is documented in the official records and when it is heard in reported speech or, more directly, through her own notes, cards, and letters. Letters written by people with learning difficulties are rare, and yet in these documents Alice's voice comes through clearly.

A photograph album has added another dimension to the oral history. After Alice's death, Mrs Pearce put together a memorial album containing photographs of Alice and her friends, some of which were taken by Alice, and a collection of Birthday and Valentine cards and notes. A discussion of the photographs cannot be separated from the accompanying narrative of the owner of the album, Mrs Pearce, so I shall be combining the two. Family albums containing ordinary snapshots are now recognised as valuable historical and sociological sources, reclaiming the detail of everyday life. At the same time, it is important to remember that many albums are eulogistic epics or sagas, almost mythic, needing careful analysis and different layers of interpretation.[96] The Album works on at least two levels: its theme, as constructed by Mrs Pearce, is a memorial album made by her in honour of Alice; but its type, as produced by Alice, is above all Alice's autobiographical and family album. It gives glimpses of hostel and family life, representing aspects of the life histories of both women, and the history of their times. According to Mrs Pearce:

> *... Alice's memory is too precious to forget. She was a wonderful person ... she really was special ... Of course this [album] is mostly about Alice ... but it does give you the whole idea of the hostel in a way, doesn't it?*

As well as the memorial album there were other types of archive material which contributed to a reconstruction of Alice's life story. I have looked at documents from the Norfolk Record Office which contain the official information on the background of Alice's life, and on the development of community care.

Figure 9 - The Girls' Orphanage, Norwich, circa 1905

In telling Alice's story, therefore, I have used many sources, including the voices of those who knew Alice. Without these various historical sources there would be no life-story: without the mediated oral history from Mrs Pearce, no written biography of Alice would exist, and an opportunity to learn more about early twentieth-century policy concerning learning disability from a specific life story would be lost.

The life history: border controls and the first crossing
Alice's life had at least eight major border crossings into and out of institutions and community care, and finally 'out into the world', and I discuss some of the most important ones. She was born in 1897 in the Norwich Poor Law Institution and sent as a small child to the Girls' Orphanage in Norwich. The oral history evidence gives an insight into her life in the Orphanage. She told Mrs Pearce that she was very unhappy, 'She hated it there, hated it!' She said that it was during her time in care that she had her ears boxed so hard that she began to lose her hearing, and quite soon became very deaf. The devastating result of this abuse seems to have been not only a physical disability – in 1912 the decision was taken to send her away at the age of fifteen to Stoke Park Colony in Bristol.

Whether this decision was taken because she was high-spirited and a rebel, or because of her inability to hear clearly, is difficult to say, but there is evidence that young female orphans, in particular, who were thought to be disruptive, and who were in the charge of Industrial Schools or the Society for Waifs and Strays, were some-times certified. This was seen as one way of removing 'problem' cases. Pamela Cox found that, 'girls were much more likely to be seen as 'defective' if it was thought that they would be difficult to place in service or to adjust to the role of demure domestic servant.'[97] Mrs Pearce said that Alice was always 'high spirited ... a leader'. In the group photograph of the orphans, most of the girls are sitting demurely cross-legged, but Alice in the front row has her legs stuck out defiantly in front of her, striking a non-conforming pose despite the ribbons and the collars (Figure 9). The main route out of the orphanage for the girls, some as young as twelve or fourteen, was into domestic service. If the Guardians anticipated that Alice was going to be difficult to place, they might well have sought to give the 'problem' to someone else.

The first border crossing 220 miles away from Norwich was momentous. It meant that she lost rights and freedom and was effectively controlled and directed from that date for most of the rest of her life by the Mental Deficiency authorities. While in the orphanage she had had the chance of an ordinary life. She now had a label and, after 1913, was to become 'subject to be dealt with' under the Mental Deficiency Act. She was excluded from ordinary life, and deprived of opportunities for employment, independence and family life.

Behind this decision to send Alice away were various aspects of national and local policy. The atmosphere in which it could happen was influenced by the National Association for Promoting the Welfare of the Feebleminded, founded the year before Alice was born, and also the views of the Eugenics Society, formed in 1907. At national level, the Mental Deficiency Act was about to be passed in 1913. This act urged that people with learning difficulties should be controlled and segregated, either in isolated colonies, or in the community by means of strict supervision in families. As there was no local colony in Norfolk, many people, like Alice, were 'discovered' or 'ascertained' by local Enquiry Officers, and sent instead to institutions all over the country, as far afield as Bristol and Liverpool, in a programme of large scale and hidden migration. The local authorities kept in touch at intervals with the people they sent out of the county. This is a report by the Norwich Enquiry Officer after a visit to Stoke Park in 1921 when Alice had been there nine years:

> ... *all very fat and well, and the girls much grown. Stoke Park is an immense place, the estate comprising over 1,100 acres, and the Institution consisting of 10 separate houses – the total number of patients being 1,557. There are no vacancies and we feel there must be immense demand when they occur.*[98]

The Officers did not always see the reality of certain aspects of life at the colony. Alice told Mrs Pearce that Stoke Park was 'awful, terrible' and that she had to scrub steps every day, '... scrub them till they were as white as snow'. Mrs Pearce told me that Alice rarely spoke of her time at Stoke Park, and when she did, it was to describe the hard work, for which she was not paid, and to say how much she hated it there. Many people have told of similar experiences in institutions in the 1920s and 1930s, of the punishments, and of the endless 'scrubbing', which took up so much of their lives.[99] These punishing tasks may have been part of an imposed preparation for the time when another transition could be made. Alice's language to describe her work seems to symbolise the idea of redemption, to become 'as white as snow'. It may be that she had to make up for her rebelliousness by extra scrubbing duties, and that these represented an atonement to be paid to society, a way of gaining redemption before she could cross borders once more.

Return to Norwich: 'mingling' in the borderlands

After nineteen years at Stoke Park Colony, Alice made another border crossing when, on January 9, 1930, at the age of 34, she was brought back to Norwich and placed in Eaton Grange, a newly opened hostel for women with learning difficulties. Three reasons for her return begin to emerge. The first is related to both national and local policy. National policy after the first world war meant that local authorities were urged to open further institutions for people with learning difficulties. The Board of Control kept up constant pressure on Norwich and Norfolk to do so, until eventually in 1929 they started to look for suitable buildings for a hostel and a colony, both of which were opened in 1930. A second reason given for Alice's return was a realisation that the policy of sending people out of the county was inhumane. In a speech made at the opening of the hostel by the Deputy Lord Mayor, he said, 'To send people miles away where the parents could not see them, appeared to be almost an act of tyranny.'[100] It was also becoming expensive for Norwich Borough Council to have to use distant institutions – 15s 9d a week was paid to keep Alice at Stoke Park – whereas the hostel could benefit from any money she might earn if she went out to work.[101]

This was a major border crossing for Alice. The hostel was in the city rather than in an isolated position like Stoke Park, and although she was still detained under the Mental Deficiency Acts and monitored by the Board of Control, the oral history and the photographs paint a more complex picture. The life they describe reveals a blurring of the borderlands, in which Alice is included in some aspects of ordinary life, yet still excluded from others.

There are, not surprisingly, no photographs of Stoke Park Colony in Alice's memorial album, but several mark her return to Norwich. A formal photograph of the Matron of the hostel contrasts with a scene of the day at the seaside, with the Matron in the middle of, and indistinguishable from, the group of laughing women residents from the hostel. Mrs Pearce knew the Matron as a family friend and she described her own perception of life at the hostel in the early 1940s:

> *They were happy ... all the women I had any contact with ... they loved it at the hostel ... they couldn't talk highly enough about the Matron and about the Nurses. And the Matron, she was like a Queen ... they worshipped her ... she knew how to keep the rule, but she was really good. Yes. Isn't she somewhere there at the back? You can see from this little snap the happiness of the girls, can't you?*

In this interplay of image and narrative, the narrator called on the photograph to bear witness to the truth of what she was saying. In her own report on the day, the Matron said:

> *Last summer, arrangements were made for all to have a day at the seaside, which was to be a never-to-be-forgotten experience of those whose opportunities to share in seaside delights have been a negligible quantity.*[102]

Other reports by the Matron described the 'happy family atmosphere' of the hostel: tennis, cricket and 'town parole', concerts, and free seats at the cinema, dancing till midnight at Christmas time, and friends invited to the hostel for tea. She described it as 'the eldorado' for the women brought back to Norwich from colonies or Poor Law Institutions, an ideal echoed by the Sheriff in a speech made at a hostel garden fete. He said that the women were now able to experience:

> *... the joys of real home life and the joy of mingling with those who had full use of their liberty.*[103]

The rhetoric and the glowing reports do, however, have to be treated with some caution. The photograph of the day at the seaside captured, I have discovered from the records, the one day at the seaside a year that the women were allowed, funded from the proceeds of the annual fete. There is evidence from the records and other oral history interviews that the hostel did have an institutional regime which was not always as relaxed as it appears in these descriptions and these images. By comparison with their previous lives, however, the hostel must have seemed to the women a most dramatic change, a border crossed indeed, and the chance of a new life.

'Pleased at the opportunity to earn her own living'

The records show that Alice was almost immediately found a place of work outside the hostel, and went out on licence on a daily basis to do domestic work. This was another border crossed, and she was moving further and further out of official control. The Matron recorded Alice's daily life:

> *After having a cup of tea with bread and butter, Alice goes at 7.30 a.m., returning at 6 p.m.; helping with any needlework in the afternoon. Mrs F. (Alice's new employer) has agreed to pay Alice 2 /- per week with meals; also 4 /- per week to the Institution which Mrs F. will pay to the City Accountant.*

And for the first time we hear Alice's own voice reported, 'Alice is very happy and comfortable; also, pleased at the opportunity to earn her own living.'[104]

The pattern of Alice's working life at this point illustrates the local policy decisions that had been made when the hostel was established. The Town Clerk, prompted by the Medical Officer, had emphasised that, 'it is hoped to develop the hostel idea, with some going out to daily employment.'[105] Hostels had the dual role of enabling community contact, within strict limits and controls. As early as 1923 Evelyn Fox, the Secretary of the Central Association for Mental Welfare, had suggested the provision of 'working hostels' as part of what she called 'a living community service',[106] and in 1930 she was calling hostels, 'an integral part of community control'.[107] Although Matron said that 'some of the girls (sic) are allowed out alone, which helps them to feel that they really belong to the outside world',[108] in fact contacts with the outside world were to be monitored, in line with the national policy of 'care and control'. The Wood Report of 1929, and the 1927 Act, both called for the further development of community control as well as care, with duties of licence, supervision and monitored guardianship. The rhetoric of 'belonging' was belied by the difficulties still put in the way of joining society, and not everyone was granted membership. In this border-land, Alice was 'mingling'; at this point in her life, she was at the same time in the community, but not part of it.

Figure 10 – Alice in Mrs F.'s Garden

Figure 11 - Alice Chapman

As her experience of daily domestic work proved successful, Alice's life began to change very quickly. In 1931 she left the hostel altogether to go out on licence to live in with Mrs F. where, the records say, she 'receives 6/- a week and is self-supporting and has given every satisfaction'.[109] Alice later told Mrs Pearce that she had enjoyed her new job. There is an informality in the group of photographs documenting this border crossing which seems to confirm this, or at the very least documents new experiences for Alice as she relaxes in the garden (Figure 10), or cradles a kitten. A snapshot of her employer was kept by Alice in her own collection, and so must represent a significant memory. An image of Alice as an elegant 'woman about town', with hat and suit, seems, like a first passport photograph, to symbolise new rights and a new membership of the community, a signing up to 'the outside world' (Figure 11). In a speech before local sponsors and dignitaries, the Matron used Alice's story to exemplify the success and progress of the hostel:

> *Whilst away from home in Stoke Park no opportunity*
> *presented itself for her to be given the chance amongst her*
> *more fortunate friends in civil life. After only a short stay at*
> *the hostel she [Alice] has now been able to go out into service for*
> *the first time to a freedom which has hitherto been unknown to*
> *her.*[110]

Alice, who had been sent away from Norwich because she was thought to be unemployable, had become the success story of the early years of the hostel.

'Cocoa upstairs for two'. And Alice came too: a caring role as pass-port to the community

On the death of Mrs F., her first employer, Alice did not return to the hostel, but went to live first with Mrs Pearce's mother, and then with Mrs Pearce herself as a live-in domestic. She remained with her and her family for twenty years, becoming friend and confidante, child and granny-carer, and on occasions running the household. According to Mrs Pearce:

> When Mrs F. died, and my mother was widowed, Matron said, 'Well, probably Alice would be a good one to come to you ... for company...', so she came and lived with my mother. She became quite a good cook. Used to make a lovely stew! They used to work together to keep the house going, and she used to go out and have her various activities, with the Chapel and the various friends she's made.

When Mrs Pearce's mother became ill and had to move in with Mrs Pearce,

> Alice came too. She took it for granted. For a year we all looked after my mother. Alice was a great help ...

The idea that 'Alice came too' as a matter of course, represents an almost seamless transition and one that Alice wanted to make – 'she took it for granted'. This extended family also became Alice's family with affection on both sides, and her caring role within it seems to have been her choice and not her burden, a role that became her passport into community life. Jan Walmsley has written about the importance of revealing the unknown caring roles of women with learning difficulties 'to correct the view of them as purely dependent, disregarded, and excluded, and to ensure them a place in the world'.[111] On one occasion when Mrs Pearce was away, Alice took over many of her duties and described them in a letter:

> ... the boys have been very good, and Mr Pearce has looked after me for meals, and I have cooked up for them for supper. I am keeping OK and doing my best, have managed to have good drying days for washing. I miss you when I make a cup of tea. Take as much rest as you can while you have the chance.

Figure 12 - A page from the Memorial Album

She baby-sat for the family, and wrote many affectionate cards and notes which Mrs Pearce kept and placed in the album. They seem to confirm the pleasure and pride Alice took in her life and work with this family (Figure 12).

The photographs of this time (Figure 13) and the narrative that described the events, seem to imply that in most aspects of her life, Alice was now no longer excluded. Family holiday snapshots illustrate that she was by now doing more than 'mingling'; she was an accepted member of the community. Mrs Pearce said:

> *Those women who went out from Eaton Grange were part of the families they were helping ... she [Alice] used to have her holidays down at Bacton with my aunt and uncle who used to have a boarding house – look, there she is – and she loved that ... There are all the guests, and she used to love to be with them ... there are all the holiday-makers.*

and

> *Alice would be fairly free, you know, it was just home really to her. The boys loved her ... and she had a social life of her own ... there was a lot to do with Chapel – outings and things like that ... she could go out whenever she wanted.*

The relationship was portrayed as one of equals, and one of great affection on both sides, and yet it was more complex than that. The family, according to legislation – and of course Alice was still 'under the Act' – were *her* 'carers' and were 'in loco parentis', so even at the moment of inclusion into the community, the lines were blurred and her status uncertain. Until 1956, when she was finally discharged, she was still 'subject to be dealt with' under the 1913 Mental Deficiency Act. This meant that officials visited the Pearce household every four months, reviewed Alice's position every five years and continued to declare that she was 'still to be detained'. She was, according to the policy of the day still seen officially as a threat to society. At the opening of the hostel in 1930, the Lord Mayor had said:

> *If the Hostel cannot cure, may it be the means of preventing more mental defectives from being brought into the world.*[112]

In the 1950s this philosophy was still underpinning the functioning of community care. The official forms for social workers in 1953, when Alice was 56, asked:

> *Is the general supervision sufficient to minimise the risk of marriage and the procreation of children?*

I asked Mrs Pearce what Alice had felt about having her life limited in this way, and she said that she never talked about it, and seemed absolutely happy as she was, with many friends and a busy social life. But for Alice and many like her, however rosy the picture that emerges from the photographs, from Mrs Pearce's memories, and from Alice's own letters, it must be remembered that she had been prevented as a young woman from having her own family and her independence.

Final Crossing: Independence
In 1951, with their pamphlet '50,000 Outside the Law', the National Council for Civil Liberties challenged the 1913 Act on humanitarian grounds (see Chapter 7). A Royal Commission was set up in 1954, and the Mental Health Act of 1959 finally repealed the 1913 Act. Alice's own discharge from the 1913 Act in 1956 in fact did not change her life at all, as she chose to stay with Mrs Pearce and her family. This particular border crossing therefore went almost unnoticed.

She finally gained complete independence and her own home when she retired and made the last border crossing into Doughty's Hospital, a home for older people in Norwich. The last photographs in the album show Alice in the home, which, according to Mrs Pearce,

> *... she absolutely loved. I cried my eyes out the day she went ... but she loved it there. She had her own bed-sitting room, kitchen, bathroom. She enjoyed being responsible, doing her own shopping.*
>
> *She still came to visit us, and spent every Christmas with us. I always visited her when I was in Norwich.*

A letter Alice wrote to Mrs Pearce after she moved shows the strong bond between the two women, but also the delight Alice felt in her new independence:

> *Sorry I missed you this morning. I was in Stump Cross, shopping, getting in my dinner (pigs fry and veg. and a nice new loaf). I will be pleased to see you whenever you are up this end again. I have done my shopping for the weekend except Sunday joint on Saturday morning. I have done quite a lot of my rug and it looks very pretty indeed. Hope you are all well including Spot and Percy [the dogs]. I am longing to come down and be with you all again. We had a lovely Whist Party last Thursday given by Matron. Please give my love to the boys and receive the same yourself. Sorry I missed you, will be home weekend.*

Figure 13 - Alice at Great Yarmouth

A photograph of Alice taken at this time shows her standing on the beach alone (Figure 13). Mrs Pearce was the photographer, so Alice was on a day out with chosen friends. It contrasts with the earlier group photograph, taken just after her move back from Stoke Park, depicting a seaside outing from the hostel. In its image of an independent figure, the later photograph encapsulates the distance she had travelled, and the borders crossed.

Why had Alice been able to cross so many boundaries so quickly? Some of the answers lie in the fact that the authorities had begun to approve of her. Matron called her 'a well-behaved and clean woman, a willing worker, and very anxious to have a trial'. Alice had passed the test. She was redeemed. We might speculate about what would have happened to her if she had not come up to the standards required of her. Would she have been offered the same chances, so soon after her return from Stoke Park Colony, to cross the borders to a more independent life?

Some of the other women in the hostel also underwent various transitions in their lives, but with very different consequences. Marion Green had to contend with more stringent border controls and ultimately was debarred altogether from rejoining society. Like Alice she went out to daily domestic work from the hostel; unlike Alice, this was never transformed into a live-in job with a surrogate family. As Alice's life has shown, for the women living in the hostel, work meant more than a pay packet; it was a progression route incorporating various stages which could lead out of the hostel and towards an ordinary life. The surveillance and border controls set in place by the 1913 Act, however, prevented some of the women, including Marion, from taking this route. She has some good memories of the hostel life, but she rebelled against the restrictions and the rules. Unlike Alice, Marion did not conform; she was a younger woman – only 22 – when she arrived at the hostel in 1943 and felt constrained by the detention. Her family also fought on her behalf and according to Marion, 'My mother wanted me home'. Under the Mental Deficiency Act, families were scrutinised for their ability to control their children, and the official decision as to whether they could supervise their daughter or son was often tainted by class and gender beliefs. Although Marion, unlike Alice, did have a family to support her so that negotiations could take place over these border crossings, her family in the end was judged unsuitable and was therefore powerless to change the situation. Whereas Alice had been described as 'well-behaved', Marion did not often pass this test. She continued to claim her rights to an ordinary life. Alice, on the other hand, having been through the experience of Stoke Park, conformed in the end to the role of domestic servant expected of her. She was lucky enough to find congenial families to work for and to find a role she could play in their lives.

Conclusion

Dorothy Atkinson has suggested that 'the individual life story, and the collections of various life stories, can begin to challenge the many myths which surround people with learning difficulties' and encourage 'a greater historical awareness and understanding of past events'.[114] Jean Andrews says that her life story 'can let people know what I've been through ... That is important'.[115] A multiplicity of voices can illuminate the great variety of experiences of institutional and community care and the early history of learning disability.

When Alice and Marion were excluded from society in 1912 and 1943 respectively, their paths crossed not only county boundaries but metaphorical boundaries between freedom and control. Alice's life story, and the counterpoint of some of Marion's very different experiences, illustrate some of the reasons why the two women, contemporaries for some time in the hostel, nevertheless took different routes in the end. Luck, an ability to conform and the discovery of a caring role, played a part in Alice's transitions; Marion on the other hand felt constrained by the hostel regulations and fought against them. What we learn from analysing the memorial album is that Alice's voice begins to emerge and to be acknowledged at various important transitions, and that far from being solely a victim, she was able to begin to influence the steps she would take towards an ordinary life.

---

[93] David Sibley, *Geographies of Exclusion. Society and Difference in the West,* (London: Routledge, 1995).

[94] Jan Walmsley, *Gender, Caring and Learning Disability,* (Unpublished PhD thesis, Open University, 1994), p.180.

[95] I have also written about the life of Alice Chapman in 'Enforced Migrations by People with Learning Difficulties: A Case Study', *Oral History,* (Spring 1999), 47-56.

[96] Andrew Walker and Rosalind Moulton, 'Photo Albums : Images of Time and Reflections of Self', *Qualitative Sociology,* 12(2), (Summer 1989), 164-165.

[97] Pamela Cox, 'Girls, deficiency and delinquency', in Wright, D. and Digby, A. (eds), *From Idiocy to Mental Deficiency: Historical Perspectives on people with learning difficulties,* (London: Routledge, 1996).

[98] Report of a visit to Stoke Park Colony, October, 1921, *Mentally Defective (care of) Committee,* Norfolk Record Office, N/TC/18/1.

[99] For example, see Margaret's story in Dorothy Atkinson, *An Auto/Biographical Approach to Learning. Disability Research,* (Aldershot: Ashgate, 1997), p.91.

[100] Speech made by the Deputy Lord Mayor at the opening ceremony for Eaton Grange (Eastern Daily Press, 24 September, 1930).

[101] Clerk's Report regarding maintenance charges at Stoke Park Colony, June 7, 1923, Norfolk Record Office, N/TC 18/1.

[102] Matron's Report, October 1931, *Norwich Mental Deficiency Committee,* Norfolk Record Office, N/TC/52/41.

[103] *Eastern Daily Press,* Norwich, 1 July, 1932.

[104] Matron's Report, October 1931, *Norwich Mental Deficiency Committee*, Norfolk Record Office, Norfolk Record Office, N/TC/52/41.

[105] Letter from the Town Clerk to the Board of Control, 16th March 1930, *Norwich Mental Deficiency Committee,* Norfolk Record Office, N/TC/52/41.

[106] Evelyn Fox, 'The Mentally Defective and the Community', in *Studies in Mental Deficiency,* Central Association for Mental Welfare, 4 (4), (October 15, 1923) pp.74 and 77.

[107] Evelyn Fox, 'Community Schemes for the Social Control of Mental Defectives', in *Mental Welfare,* 11(3) (July 15, 1930), p.68.

[108] A speech given by the Matron at an Open Evening at Eaton Grange, 21 March 1932, Norfolk Record Office, N/TC/52/41.

[109] Matron's Report on patients on licence, January 1933, Norfolk Record Office, N/TC/52/41.

[110] A speech given by the Matron at an Open Evening at Eaton Grange, 21 March 1932, Norfolk Record Office, N/TC/52/41

[111] Jan Walmsley, 'Contradictions in Caring : Reciprocity and Interdependence', *Disability, Handicap and Society*, 8(2), (1993), 129-141.

[112] Speech made by the Lord Mayor at the opening ceremony for Eaton Grange (*Eastern Daily Press*, 24 September 1930).

[113] Matron's Report, September 1931, Norfolk Record Office, N/TC/52/41.

[114] Dorothy Atkinson, *An Auto/Biographical Approach,* pp.11-12.

[115] Jean Andrews, 'Scrub, scrub, scrub ... bad times and good times: some of the jobs I've done in my life', in *Good Times, Bad Times: Stories by Women with Learning Difficulties*, (Kidderminster: BILD, 2000).

Chapter 7

Equal citizens?
The discourse of liberty and rights in the history of learning disabilities

Tim Stainton

Summary

In this chapter Tim Stainton considers the boundary that debars people with learning difficulties[116] from equal citizenship. He briefly considers the nature of this boundary and then looks at two examples where it was temporarily challenged. The first is concerned with the 1913 Mental Deficiency Act and the opposition to it by Josiah Wedgwood. The second example deals with the National Council For Civil Liberties' campaign, in the early 1950s, to reform the Mental Deficiency Laws. In the chapter, he argues that both of these struggles were based on a general concern with individual liberty and rights. Finally, he suggests that this should be the basis of the current campaign for equal citizenship.

Introduction

In recent years the language of rights, liberty and citizenship has become common in the discourse around learning disabilities. This is a discourse which has been at the heart of modern western society since the enlightenment, a discourse from which people with learning difficulties have been consciously and explicitly excluded. The boundary which separates the equal citizen from the *other* has proved to be one of the most intractable which people with learning difficulties must cross, but cross they must if they are ever to achieve the rights, liberty and equality which the vast majority of citizens take for granted. This chapter is part of the story of that journey. I shall consider the nature of the boundary, and two examples of where a discursive breach in the barrier was made. Finally, I will briefly consider what lessons these two examples might have for the current debate.

'Civil death': the denial of rights

The exclusion of people thought to lack a certain type or degree of reason from equal citizenship has a long history. Its early roots can be traced back to ancient Greece where Aristotle argued that slaves and women were 'naturally' inferior on the basis that they did not possess, or at least not to a sufficient degree, reason,[117] and so were justifiably excluded from equal citizenship. The Stoics associated moral responsibility with the giving of a rational account and the Epicureans argued that justice only extends to those capable of making a contract.[118]

The same ideas resurfaced in the enlightenment and forged the basis of the moral and political position of people with learning difficulties in modern western democracies. John Locke was clear that participation in the liberal state was contingent upon reason. In his *Two Treatises of Government* he states:

> But if through defects that may happen out of the ordinary course of Nature, any one comes not to such a degree of reason wherein he might be supposed capable of knowing the law ... he is never capable of being a free man ... So lunatics and idiots are never set free from the government of their parents.[119]

Samuel Pufendorf, another natural law theorist, noted: 'To make a

Man capable of (I) giving a ferious and firm *Confent*, tis above all things necessary that he be mafter of his Reafon.' He went on to state that if one is incurably lacking in reason then he 'is in all Legal and Moral Confideration to be accounted *Dead*'. The latter reference is to the notion of *civil death*, an exclusion from society and civil life.[120]

This view, that some specific degree or type of reason is a prerequisite for equal rights and citizenship, has resulted in their denial to people with learning difficulties and others throughout the modern history of western society. The definition of those considered to lack this imagined degree of reason has expanded and contracted, at times embracing women, non-white ethnic groups, the poor and, inevitably and virtually continuously, those considered to have a learning disability. It is on this basis that both the smothering blanket of paternalism and the atrocities of control, elimination and seg-regation have been justified. While the struggle for inclusion in the company of rights-bearing citizens has been most evident in recent years, examples of earlier attempts to include people with learning difficulties within this discourse can be found. Below I consider two such examples.

Josiah Wedgwood and the 1913 Mental Deficiency Bill

The first example comes from what is arguably one of the darkest periods in the history of people considered to have some form of learning disability. As Thomson argues, the early twentieth century in Britain saw a recognition of the state's duty to support citizens to overcome external barriers to self-improvement and development of moral character. However, contemporary with this development was the view that those with mental defects were biologically incapable of wilful self-improvement. This biological division 'led to the exclusion of mental defectives from the contract of citizenship rights and responsibilities which lay at the heart of the liberal British polity'.[121] As the above suggests, this was not a new state of affairs in itself, but the wedding of this long standing belief with the scientism of eugenics gave it an added poignancy at this point.

The advent of eugenics in the mid 1860s rapidly led to an increase in calls for 'something to be done about the "feebleminded"' to prevent the imminent deterioration of the race. 1896 saw the first lobby group specifically concerned with learning disability, the National Association for Promoting the Welfare of the Feebleminded (NAPWF), an offshoot of the Charity Organisation Society.[122] The goals of this group were anything but ambiguous. At a meeting of the association Lord Herschell moved a resolution affirming that:

> *The existence of large classes of feeble-minded persons is a danger to the moral and physical welfare of society and calls for immediate attention both on the part of public authorities and charitable enterprise.*[123]

Agitation by the NAPWF, concern among prison and poor law authorities, and the increasing public concern with 'degeneration' led to the appointment in 1904 of the *Royal Commission on the Care and Control of the Feeble-Minded*.[124] The Commission sat for four years, hearing 248 witnesses, and undertook its own investigations. The voluminous *Report and Minutes of Evidence* provide a fascinating compilation of contemporary, and often contradictory, views of 'mental deficiency'[125] which, Jones suggested, steered a sane course between the 'Scylla of "liberty of the subject" and the Charybdis of eugenics theory'.[126] What is more accurate is that the *Report* captured the transition from a period of relatively humane paternalism to active suppression and control.

The Commission undertook an extensive survey of the numbers of 'mental defectives' both in the community and in various institutions (workhouses, asylums, prisons etc.). It concluded:

> *... besides those who are already recognized...we have placed ... other groups of persons not hitherto ... recognized as such in law ... These groups include imbeciles, feeble-minded persons, moral imbeciles ...*[127]

> *... there are numbers of mentally defective persons whose training is neglected, over whom no sufficient control is exercised, and whose wayward and irresponsible lives are productive of crime and misery, of much injury to themselves and to others, and of much continuous expenditure wasteful to the community and to individual families ...*[128]

In its ninety-six recommendations it covers almost every aspect of regulating people thought to have a mental deficiency. In short, the report expanded the definition of 'who' the mentally defective were and firmly established the role of the state in the classification, identification and regulation of people thought to have a mental deficiency. Despite its paternal overtones, the Commission laid the groundwork for the systematic repression by the state of this putative class of persons.

Calls for a Bill to follow-up the 1908 Royal Commission became increasingly vociferous, led by the NAPWF and the newly formed Eugenics Education Society (ESS). The increasing strength and prevalence of hereditarian claims fuelled calls for government action. Searle notes that 'there could have been few towns of any size which did not hold a public meeting in the 1909–1913 period, to protest the Government's passivity in the face of the "menace of the feeble-minded".[129] Both the Minority and Majority Poor Law Commission (1905-9) reports supported action on segregation,[130] and Freeden notes the lively debate in the press and the division on the issue among liberals.[131]

There was also support within the Liberal government, particularly from Winston Churchill, Home Secretary from February 1910 to October 1911. He warned Asquith of 'a very terrible danger to the race' and said that, until the public came to accept sterilisation, segregation from the community and between the sexes was required. He also circulated with approval an alarmist address given by Tredgold to cabinet colleagues.[132]

A joint effort by the NAPWF and ESS resulted in the formation of a committee of MPs to oversee the introduction of a private members Bill drafted by the lobbyist. The Bill passed its second reading and succeeded in getting the government to introduce its own Bill in May of 1912. The *Mental Deficiency Bill* included clauses which 'defined the feeble-minded as incapable of competing on equal terms with their normal fellows' or 'of managing themselves and their affairs with ordinary prudence'.[133] It also included a clause which made it a misdemeanour to marry a mental defective.[134] This Bill was allowed to lapse but was reintroduced in March of 1913 with the most obviously eugenic measures removed.

The Bill defined four types of 'mental defective': idiots, imbeciles, feeble-minded, and moral imbeciles; and provided for a person who fitted into one of the four broad categories to be:

... sent or placed in an institution for defectives or placed under guardianship:

(a) at the insistence of his parent or guardian, if he is an idiot or imbecile or is under the age of twenty-one; or

(b) if in addition to being a defective he is a person:

> (i) who is found neglected, abandoned, or without visible means of support, or cruelly treated; or
> (ii) who is found guilty of a criminal offense ...
> (iii) who is undergoing imprisonment ... or penal servitude ... who is an habitual drunkard ...
> (v) in whose case notice has been given by the local education authority ...
> (vi) who is in receipt of poor relief at the time of giving birth to an illegitimate child or when pregnant of such child.[135]

Certification was made by two physicians, initially for one year, and then for five year periods if the Board of Control considered it to be 'in the interest of the defective'.[136]

On 30 July 1913, after a remarkable filibuster by Josiah Wedgwood who fought the Bill 'through two all night sittings, sustained on chocolate',[137] putting up 120 amendments and making 150 speeches,[138] the Bill passed with only Wedgwood and two others opposed.[139] This Bill set the stage for the expansion of large institutional facilities[140] and the dominance of the state over the lives of people with learning difficulties. With this Bill, to all intents and purposes, it became a crime to have a learning disability.

Wedgwood, who had no particular interest in 'mental deficiency', opposed the 1912 and 1913 Bills, and his own party, explicitly on the issue of individual liberty.[141] Jones paints a picture of Wedgwood as inconsistent and misguided, suggesting that, 'In retrospect, one might wish that such a champion might have a better cause'.[142] However, it is striking, on reading over the transcripts of the debate, just how astute many of his criticisms and fears were.[143] Commenting on the 1912 Bill, Wedgwood sums up fairly accurately what was to be the case: 'there is perpetual imprisonment writ large all over the Bill.'[144] And on the 1913 Bill he notes 'if this Bill is passed into law, it will put into prison 100,000 people who are at present at liberty',[145] a figure not far off what would become the reality. Women considered to be of 'immoral character' would be particularly vulnerable as recent biographical work on those committed under the Act shows.[146]

Speaking against the 1912 Bill, Wedgwood put the case for justice and rights in compelling terms:

> *... this Bill, ... is based upon that Report. The Royal Commission [of 1908] consisted of specialists, many of them members of the Eugenics Society, all of them people who have one aim and object ... the materialistic one of improving the race and the breed of people in this country. I submit our object as politicians in a democratic country is not ... to breed the working classes ... Our object ... is to secure justice for everybody .... It seems the Commission concentrated throughout on the materialistic side, and not on ... human rights as coming before human advantages.*[147]

On the 1913 Bill, Wedgwood took up the issue of 'expertise', citing the vagueness of the definitions and the non-medical nature of many of the judgements required and despite the limited safeguards in the Bill, how in practice 'it will be fatally easy to get these certificates'.[148] He repeatedly attacked the 'eugenics cranks' and warned of the 'growing authority of the specialist over the liberty of the individual'.[149] Again a prescient judgement on what was to come.[150]

Wedgwood returned to the fray in 1926 wrecking the first amendment Bill and later commenting on the Bill which eventually became the 1927 Mental Deficiency Act:

> *However excellent your institution may be, however carefully you may select the matrons and managers in charge, so long as you have locks on the door, you cannot prevent the suspicion of those minor cruelties, injustices and acts of arbitrary authority which may embitter the life of the inmates of these institutions. Once you have gotten rid of the lock, why then, your institutions, even without so much inspection, will improve, because freedom- publicity- is the cure for inhumanity and injustice.*[151]

It should be noted that Wedgwood was not against support. On the contrary, he was quite vocal in advocating voluntary homes and colonies and called for more funds to be channelled to them. His concern was with the coercive nature of the provisions and with the use of private facilities for profit. While some of his suggestions may not meet with total approval today, he painted a very positive picture of how people should be supported and at no time questioned their right to liberty or their moral status as equal people.[152]

As the above clearly demonstrates, Wedgwood's concern was primarily with the liberty and rights of the person, not with mental deficiency. What is remarkable, given the times, is that he was not inclined to see them as being 'outside the bounds of justice', as many of his progressive contemporaries were. Although shrouded in eugenic fear-mongering and scientism, this was a fight for individual liberty and the rights of the putative class of 'mental defectives' to equal citizenship and freedom.[153] Beveridge, who was a eugenics supporter at this time, let the game slip somewhat when he wrote that those who, 'through "general defects" were unable to fill the social role of a complete person ought to be regarded as "unemployable" and so as the dependants of the state; they should be maintained in public institutions and lose all their rights as citizens including the franchise, civil freedom, and fatherhood.'[154] This illustrates both the association of 'competence' and rights, and the belief that when one requires state supports and services, rights must be exchanged for the privilege. This has been and remains a common feature of welfare systems.[155]

Wedgwood was a rather enigmatic character, switching from the Liberals to Labour, and as often as not voting against rather than for his own party. His career, though unremarkable in terms of achievement, was marked by this passionate defence of liberal principles which he saw no reason to discard because of a particular label that was attached to an individual. His own rationale for his famous filibuster on the 1913 Bill was that his wife had left him and he was 'very nearly off his head'.[156] However the fact that he fought consistently against the original 1912 Bill through to the 1927 Bill suggests a more plausible answer lies in his lifelong commitment to liberty, regardless of the label.[157]

The National Council for Civil Liberties and the Royal Commission of 1954–57

The second example comes from the reaction to the outcomes of the 1913 Act, many of which Wedgwood had accurately predicted. The horrors of the Nazi holocaust lessened the currency of the eugenic argument and a new concern with conditions in mental hospitals emerged which again centred on the issue of liberty.[158] In 1947 the *National Council for Civil Liberties* (NCCL) launched a campaign against the current mental deficiency regime.[159] In 1951 they published a pamphlet entitled *50,000 Outside The Law*,[160] in which they noted that 'in less than 40 years a bureaucracy has established itself in this field (mental deficiency), interpreting the law as it pleases and answerable to itself alone. Such a development is a challenge to democracy and a challenge which a democracy cannot afford to ignore.'[161] Using numerous case studies they showed how even the draconian powers to control embodied in the 1913 Act were made worse by an arrogant and isolated bureaucratic machinery which wielded the powers vested in the Act. The foreword indicates how grave they felt the situation was: 'The cases of detention under the Mental Deficiency Laws reported in this pamphlet will come as a shock to all ... The situation in the Mental Deficiency Service constitutes ... one of the gravest social scandals of the twentieth century.'[162] They raised issues about the lack of legal safeguards for people in institutions and a number of related concerns. Their efforts were a major impetus for the setting up of the Royal Commission on Law Relating to Mental Illness and Mental Deficiency 1954–1957. In their evidence to the Commission they decried the lack of education and training facilities within the institutions and the fact that what training occurred was aimed more at supporting institutional maintenance than preparation for a return to community employment. They wrote that, 'the institution is so dependent on patient labour that even if the Medical Superintendent believed that a large number of high-grade patients were qualified for release, it would be impossible for release to be granted without bringing the institution to a standstill.'[163] All of this is very reminiscent of the Minority Report on the Poor Laws in 1904 which argued that:

> *We think we are not wrong in attributing the retention of these 60,000 mentally defective persons in the Workhouses to the*

fact that their labour is found useful ... 'if' said an objector, 'you remove the feeble-minded women from the workhouse who will do the scrubbing?'[164]

The NCCL went on to note that 'Not only is a mental defective under orders deprived of his liberty and of the opportunity of obtaining an education ... but the standards of care, protection and health facilities often leave much to be desired.'[165] One primary concern was the abuse and misuse of the licence and guardianship system. They cited long periods on licence which left the person's liberty at the superintendent's discretion, and cases of abuse by employers which individuals were afraid to report for fear they would not be granted their freedom.[166] They also noted the extreme control which the institution exerted over the life and liberty of its inmates, including regulation of visitors and imposition of standard dress in institutional 'costumes'. Finally, they cited numerous cases of 'wrongful detention' under current law.[167]

In their summing up they explicitly rejected the old eugenic arguments for detention[168] and set out a series of principles for service which would not be out of place in a contemporary community care proposal:

(a) As far as possible, the services which exist for the normal citizens who need special help of any kind, should be used to provide for the mental deficients. Where special services become necessary, they should exist as departments of the appropriate general service. The provision of all such facilities to be made compulsory and not left to the discretion of the local and central authorities. Conditions within such services should be at least as good as those for people in comparable services for other sections of the community.

(b) ... A wide variety of both day and residential services should be made available and the closest liaison should exist between the specialist services and the school, the family doctor and the rehabilitation services of the Ministry of Labour.

(c) Financial assistance should be based on the principle of need and should not be in the hands of the administration of the service.[169]

Their final paragraph stated in moving terms what they saw as the appropriate response of a civilised society:

> *The idiot, the imbecile and feeble-minded are an integral part of the human race; their existence constitutes an unspoken demand on us. The extent to which we guard their right to the fullest and most useful life, the extent to which we guarantee to them the maximum freedom which they can enjoy and the extent to which we help their families to give them the love they need, is a measure of the extent to which we ourselves are civilized.*[170]

The main recommendations of the Commission included improved procedures and safeguards regarding admission and discharge, expansion of welfare and aftercare services, expansion of community based residential and training facilities, the making of the above a positive duty of local authorities rather than a permissible one, and the limiting of the hospital's role to more acute and severe cases. The legislative outcome, the Mental Health Act of 1959, would be considerably weaker, but the Commission and particularly the work of the NCCL, represented the beginning of the contemporary rights discourse. As with the previous example, the impetus came not from specialist organisations, but from one concerned first and foremost with the rights and liberties of the person. As with Wedgwood, there is no suggestion that the fact that people were labelled 'mentally deficient' reduced or mitigated their basic claim to liberty, rights and citizenship.

As Thomson notes, the NCCL's concern was primarily with the 'high grade defectives'[171] but was firmly rooted in the idea of liberty. The emergence of the welfare state and the idea of 'social citizenship' certainly contributed to the relative success of the campaign, but on the whole, the general belief that the mental defective was excluded from citizenship persisted and may in fact have worsened under the welfare state.[172] While this may have been the case, it serves as an indicator of what remains to be accomplished in terms of extending the boundary of citizenship to include all those with learning difficulties. The basis of the above campaign also indicates the grounds upon which such a campaign must be waged, that is, as with Wedgwood before, on the grounds of an all-inclusive liberty which does not recognise a divide, biological or otherwise, between the citizen and the *other*.

Conclusion

This chapter has outlined two examples of how the boundary between equal citizenship and 'civil death' was challenged. In both cases the impetus was from a general concern with the rights and freedoms of the person, not a special concern with a labelled population. Today we hear much about rights and equality in policy, programme and advocacy documents, but for the most part this is an internal 'specialist debate' with little popular understanding or support. The gulf between the rhetoric of rights and the reality remains vast. The belief that somehow people with learning difficulties do not qualify as full and equal rights-bearing citizens remains deeply embedded in our laws, policy and practices.[173] The inequalities in the justice system, laws on sterilisation, and the new eugenics[174] are just some of the critical arenas where this boundary separates those labelled as learning-disabled from equal citizenship. The struggle to cross this boundary is neither simple nor easy, requiring effort on legal, practical, social and attitudinal fronts. People with learning difficulties themselves are leading this struggle now but, as the above two examples demonstrate, the fight is one that must not be just the concern of those who are oppressed nor of the 'specialist', but of all those concerned with equality, liberty and justice.

---

[116] This chapter will subsequently use historically specific language. This is rightfully offensive to many, but to use modern terms would distort history and mask the means by which oppression was often justified.

[117] Aristotle, The Politics, T. A. Sinclair (trans.), T. J. Sanders (revisions) (London: Penguin, 1981); W. W. Fortenbaugh, 'Aristotle on Slaves and Women', in Barnes, J., Schofield, M. and Sorabji, R. (eds), *Articles on Aristotle*, (London: Duckworth, 1977), pp.135-139.

[118] Richard Sorabji, *Animal Minds and Human Values: The Origins of the Western Debate,* (Ithica: Cornell University Press, 1993), pp.7-8.

[119] John Locke, *Two Treatises of Government* [1690], (London: J.M.Dent, 1924), p.145.

[120] Samuel Pufendorf, *Of the Laws of Nature and Nations (Third Edition),* Basil Kennet translator with the notes of Jean Barbeyrac, (London: 1717), p.56, fn5.

[121] M. Thomson, *The Problem of Mental Deficiency: Eugenics, Democracy and Social Policy in Britain c.1870-1959,* (Oxford: Clarendon, 1998), p.34. See also p.42. Thomson provides an excellent review of the debate around mental deficiency throughout this period and why the eugenics debate was successful in relation to mental deficiency while having little impact elsewhere.

[122] Harvey Simmons, *From Asylum to Welfare,* (Downsview: NIMR, 1982), p.53.

[123] *The Times,* June 11th, 1898, quoted in Simmons, *From Asylum To Welfare,* p.54.

[124] R. Searle, *Eugenics and Politics In Britain: 1900-1914,* (Leyden: Noordhoff, 1976), p.9.

[125] *Royal Commission on the Care and Control of the Feeble-Minded, Report,* Cmnd. 4202, VolVIII and *Minutes of Evidence,* Vols I-VIII, *Parliamentary Papers,* 1908, Vols XXXV-XXXIX.

[126] Kathleen Jones, *A History of the Mental Health Services,* (London: Routledge & Kegan Paul, 1972), p.191.

[127] *Report,* 1908, p.10.

[128] Ibid., p.3.

[129] Searle, *Eugenics,* p.110.

[130] Ibid., p.106.

[131] M. Freeden, *The New Liberalism,* (Oxford: Clarendon, 1978), pp.190-193.

[132] Noted in Searle, *Eugenics,* p.107. See also Thomson, *The Problem Of Mental Deficiency,* p.33, and Chapter 5 of this book.

[133] Great Britain, *Mental Deficiency Bill,* Commons, 1912.

[134] Searle, *Eugenics,* p.110.

[135] Great Britain, *Mental Deficiency Bill, Parliamentary Papers*, Vol. IV, (1913), p.2.

[136] *Mental Deficiency Bill* (1913), 11(2).

[137] Josiah C. Wedgwood, *Memoirs of a Fighting Life,* (London: Hutchinson, 1940), p.84.

[138] Thomson, *The Problem Of Mental Deficiency,* p.45.

[139] See C. V. Wedgwood, *The Last of the Radicals,* (London: Johnathan Cape, 1951), p.96, for a description of the filibuster which lasted through two nights.

[140] K. Jones, *A History of the Mental Health Services,* p.208; Nancy Korman and Howard Glennerster, *Hospital Closures,* (Milton Keynes: Open University Press, 1990), pp.10-11.

[141] See C.V. Wedgwood, *The Last of the Radicals,* for biographical background.

[142] K. Jones, *A History of the Mental Health Services*, p.201.

[143] See for example: *Hansard's* (Commons), June 10, 1912; May 28, 1913.

[144] *Hansard's* (Commons), June 10, 1912, p.643.

[145] *Hansard's* (Commons), May 28th, 1913, p.245.

[146] See M. Potts and R. Fido, *A Fit Person To Be Removed: Personal Accounts of Life in a Mental Deficiency Institution,* (Plymouth: Northcote House, 1991); Steve Humphries, *A Secret World Of Sex,* (London: Sidgwick and Jackson, 1988), pp.63-5. Both of these provide accounts of women who were incarcerated because they had become pregnant out of wedlock, in one case due to rape.

[147] *Hansard's* (Commons), June 10, 1912, p.644.

[148] *Hansard's* (Commons), May 28, 1913, pp. 248-50; 253.

[149] *Hansard's* (Commons), June 10, 1912, p.642.

[150] See Thomson, *The Problem Of Mental Deficiency,* p.50.

[151] Cited in Jones, *A History of the Mental Health Services,* p.216.

[152] See *Hansard's* (Commons), May 28, 1913, pp. 245-48; Letter to Asquith and his article for *The Nation* quoted in C. V. Wedgwood, *The Last of the Radicals,* pp.94-95.

[153] As Thomson notes, it was only the older liberals who supported Wedgwood; new liberals and the emerging socialist were quite comfortable with the 'biological division'. Thomson, *The Problem of Mental Deficiency,* p.47.

[154] William Beveridge, 'The problem of the unemployed'. Report of a conference held by the Sociological Society, April 4, 1906, *Sociological Papers,* iii (1907), p.327. Cited in W. H. Greenleaf, *The British Political Tradition,* Volume 1, (London: Methuen, 1983), p.274.

[155] A similar example of exclusion from citizenship related to voting rights is presented by Thomson, *The Problem Of Mental Deficiency,* pp.51-4.

[156] Wedgwood, *Memoirs of a Fighting Life,* p.85.

[157] Wedgwood's numerous writings tend toward hyperbole and flippant self-reference. His own account gives the impression that his wife had died. However C. V. Wedgwood, the distinguished historian and his niece and biographer makes it clear that she had left him. He also states, somewhat strangely, on the 1913 Bill that 'they got their Bill - and never dared to use it !', *Memoirs of a Fighting Life,* p.85. Would that he were right.

[158] Thomson, *The Problem of Mental Deficiency,* pp. 278-80.

[159] Ibid., p.280.

[160] National Council For Civil Liberties, 50,000 *Outside the Law: An examination of the treatment of those certified as mentally defective,* (London: NCCL, 1951).

[161] Ibid., p.34.

[162] Ibid., Forward.

[163] *Royal Commission On The Law Relating to Mental Illness and Mental Deficiency 1954-1957, Minutes of Evidence,* p.824.

164 Sidney and Beatrice Webb (eds.), *The Break-Up of the Poor Law: Being Part One of The Minority Report of The Poor Law Commission,* (London: Longmans, Green and Co., 1909), p.302.

165 *Minutes of Evidence,* 1954-57, p.826.

166 Ibid., pp.827-8: 832.

167 Ibid., pp.829-30: 834-7.

168 Ibid., pp.845-7.

169 Ibid., p.851.

170 Ibid., p.854.

171 Thomson, *The Problem of Mental Deficiency,* p. 284.

172 Thomson argues that the insurance base of the welfare state, whereby a safety net was to be provided until a return to self-sufficiency, excluded those who needed long term support from the postwar version of social citizenship. Thomson, *The Problem of Mental Deficiency,* pp.282-3.

173 See Tim Stainton, 'Rights and Rhetoric in Policy and Practice', in Symonds, A. and Kelly, A. (eds), *The Social Construction of Community Care,* (London: Macmillan, 1998); Tim Stainton, *Autonomy and Social Policy,* (Aldershot: Avebury, 1994).

174 Tim Stainton, 'Intellectual Disability, Difference and Oppression', in Bogdan Lesnik (ed.), Countering Discrimination in Social Work, (Aldershot: Ashgate/Arena, 1998); International League of Societies for Persons With Mental Handicap, *Just Technology?* (North York: Roeher Institute, 1994); S. Keays-Bryne, 'People With Intellectual Disability and the Criminal Justice System', in *Interaction*, 10(3), (1997); M. D. A. Freeman, 'Sterilising the Mentally Handicapped', in Freeman, M. D. A. (ed.), *Medicine, Ethics and the Law* (London: Stevens and Sons, 1988).

Chapter 8

Straddling boundaries: the changing roles of voluntary organisations, 1913–1959

Jan Walmsley

Summary

In this chapter Jan Walmsley describes two voluntary organisations that worked with people with learning difficulties and their families in the twentieth century. One was the Central Association for Mental Welfare (CAMW) which, in the first half of the twentieth century, worked with the government and local authorities to make sure that people were properly supervised. She argues that, although some of what the CAMW did benefited individuals, it did not challenge the prevailing ideas that having a learning disability was somehow shameful, and that people with learning difficulties needed close supervision, preferably in institutions. The other organisation, the National Association of Parents of Backward Children (NAPBC), later became Mencap. It was founded in 1946 and its members were the families whose sons and daughters had been found by the authorities to be 'ineducable', i.e. they would not benefit from schooling. These people did challenge the authorities. They demanded better services in the community for their children and challenged the idea that families of people with learning difficulties had something to be ashamed of. Jan argues that the NAPBC did lead to more and better community services but that neither organisation really recognised the rights of people with learning difficulties to speak for themselves, and to enjoy their own homes.

Introduction

This chapter explores the changing role of voluntary organisations in provision for people with learning difficulties in England. Two voluntary organisations stand out as having nationally significant roles in the period 1913–1959, namely the Central Association for Mental Welfare (henceforward referred to as the CAMW),[175] and its local branches, and the National Association for the Parents of Backward Children (henceforward referred to as the NAPBC),[176] later known consecutively as the National Association for Mentally Handicapped Children, the National Association for Mentally Handicapped Children and Adults, and Mencap (the Royal Society). A comparison of the two organisations illustrates how different voluntary organisations are positioned in relation to the public and private divide. Members of the CAMW acted largely as an extension of the state's machinery and subjected the private world of the family with a person with a learning disability to public gaze. The NAPBC, on the other hand, was a forum in which parents of sons and daughters with a learning disability began to represent their private interests in and to the public world. Their role was to challenge the way public services were provided and demand a better deal for members and their children.

Because the chapter ends in 1959 the comparison is in some respects unsatisfactory. The period spans the entire existence of the CAMW, while it covers only the early years of the NAPBC, and it is possible to argue that, because it is a service provider as well as a campaigning organisation, the present day Mencap has a lot more in common with the CAMW than did its predecessor. However, the period chosen is not arbitrary as it spans the era of the Mental Deficiency Acts, repealed in 1959.

The argument I will put forward is that the decline of the CAMW and the founding of the NAPBC[177] represented a boundary crossing of some significance. It symbolised a watershed in the history of voluntary organisations in the UK, from early twentieth-century voluntary organisations, like the CAMW, which sought to 'do good' from an abstract, rather lofty position, filling in gaps in state provision, to more grass roots movements which espoused an advocacy role for a major group of stakeholders, in this case the families of people with learning disabilities. In doing so, the NAPBC was both a product of changing attitudes to learning disability and a contributor to those changing attitudes. Changes in attitudes are discernible in contemporary reports. In Bedfordshire, the County Medical Officer of Health began to cite damage to the mental health of parents as an argument for more institutional places around 1949,[178] while terms like 'poor little souls' also begin to be used to describe children.[179] Similarly, in the United States, Trent has documented that the early 1950s was a time when the stigma attached to having a family member with a learning disability began to recede to the extent that US celebrities, such as the author Pearl S. Buck and the actor Roy Rogers, 'came out' as parents of a mentally retarded child.[180] The appearance of the NAPBC at this time is no coincidence.

Voluntary organisations in the history of welfare

In terms of the book's theme of 'crossing boundaries', voluntary organisations are of particular interest. There are usually seen to be four main players in the provision of what we might loosely call welfare, namely the state, the private sector, the family, and the voluntary sector.[181] Of these, the voluntary sector appears to be the most fluid, at times operating at a national level, influencing policy, and at times operating as an extension of the private sphere of the family. Thus it straddles the boundaries of the public and private, frequently mediating relationships between the two. The two voluntary organisations under scrutiny both played this boundary-straddling role, though, as I will show, they positioned themselves rather differently.

Much has been written of the role of the voluntary sector in the development of state welfare in the nineteenth, and early twentieth, centuries, enough to show that they were 'part and parcel of the fabric of the state'.[182] The voluntary sector, it has been argued, was not an alternative to the state as a provider of welfare, but an integral part of it, one of a range of 'buffer institutions'[183] which mediated between the citizen and the state. The relationship between the voluntary and statutory sectors has been called a 'moving frontier'.[184] Lewis argues that, during the nineteenth century, there was a conceptualisation of cooperation within separate spheres for the state and the voluntary sector, the state being the provider of last resort while charitable action sought to intervene to prevent destitution.[185] The way the role of voluntary organisations changed during the twentieth century can be summarised as shifting from being integral to the state's provision to being supplementary to it; it would 'influence and supplement public services but no longer aim to be the first line of defence of social service'.[186] There was a growing acceptance of direct provision by the state, with voluntary organisations having only a complementary or supplementary role – this reached its apogee in the major welfare reforms of the late 1940s. This clearing away of the role of voluntary organisations as major providers of welfare left a space for the development of organisations like the NAPBC and the Spastics Society, which sought to challenge the status quo on behalf of their self-interested members. Such a division of labour seems to have held sway until the re-thinking of welfare in the late twentieth century, with voluntary organisations emerging, along with the private sector, as alternative suppliers of services in the mixed economy of welfare, but, in contrast to the late nineteenth century, almost wholly financed by the state.

Voluntary organisations have also been seen as the medium through which women entered public life and made claims to be active citizens in the public sphere. Much has been written on the 'slippery concept'[187] of maternalism. It has been debated whether women were in it for the good of other women, or to further their own interests, and it would probably be fair to say that both motives are discernible. But for the purposes of this chapter, the role women played in the two voluntary organisations under scrutiny stands as a good illustration of the contradictory boundary-straddling role they played in the implementation of the Mental Deficiency Acts, or, in the case of the NAPBC, in promoting their demise.

The beginnings: campaigning

Both the CAMW and the NAPBC began life as campaigning organisations; the former campaigning for an extension of legislation for the 'feeble-minded', the latter campaigning for the interests of the parents and children subject to the legislation which the CAMW had done so much to promote, the Mental Deficiency Acts (1913 and 1927).

The forerunner of the CAMW, the National Association for Promoting the Welfare of the Feeble-Minded, was founded in 1896. It operated in a context in which voluntary effort had been significant in the evolution of institutions for 'idiots' and 'imbeciles', pioneering efforts like Royal Earlswood, Surrey, and the Royal Western Counties Institution, Devon. The 'discovery' of the problem of the feeble-minded around the turn of the twentieth century led to campaigns to provide for an ever growing number of perceived social misfits in which the National Association for the Care and Control of the Feeble-Minded played a significant role. Alongside the Charity Organisation Society and the Eugenics Education Society, the National Association members campaigned vigorously for legislation to deal with the problem. One of the earliest branches was the Lancashire and Cheshire Society for the Permanent Care of the Feeble-Minded (1898), the forum in which the formidable Mary Dendy made her name.[188] The Lancashire and Cheshire Society had as its constitutional aims 'to collect funds and establish an institution for the care, education and welfare of "Feeble-minded persons" and to promote the welfare of such persons'.[189] Greta Jones observes that groups such as these exercised considerable influence over the Royal Commission on the Care and Control of the Feeble-Minded (1904–8), its recommendations being almost identical to those voted in 1904 at a conference of the National Association for the Care and Control of the Feeble-Minded.[190] These recommendations did not pass in totality into legislation, but the Association's influence was considerable on legislation which imposed on people with learning disabilities considerable restrictions of liberty and consequent stigmatisation (see Chapter 7).

The NAPBC first made its appearance in 1946, more than a generation after the 1913 Mental Deficiency Act. While the CAMW had campaigned for the good of society for legislation to curb the feeble-minded – none of its membership is known to have acknowledged a relative who was 'feeble-minded' – the NAPBC was from the start an organisation of parents dedicated to improving their own lot and the lot of other families with a 'backward child'. It began, according to the official 'biography' by Victoria Shennan,[191] with a letter from the mother of a child to a magazine, *Nursery World*, describing her plight. Judy Fryd, another mother, replied saying she was determined to start an Association for such parents. Thus began one of the most significant developments in the field in the postwar era. Its primary aim, initially, was to secure for all children education appropriate to age, ability and aptitude,[192] though in 1955 this was extended to:

*... efforts to prevent the birth of handicapped children and
promoting the duty of the state to care for the mentally
handicapped.*[193]

There are indeed similarities in the acceptance that feeble-
mindedness/mental handicap are undesirable; that the birth of such
people should be prevented wherever possible; and that the state
has a duty towards them. But while the CAMW believed that
segregation was the answer, the NAPBC campaigned from the start
for more facilities in the community to avert the need for institutional
care; while the NAPBC emphasised control, the NAPBC's emphasis
was on the care side of the equation; while the National Association
for the Care and Control of the Feeble-Minded (NACCFM) took an
objective quasi-scientific stance to a perceived social problem, the
NAPBC's position was subjective and partisan.

Relationships with the State

Both voluntary organisations had to develop relationships with the
state. This section compares and contrasts them in that respect.

The CAMW rapidly developed a quasi-official status after 1913.
The role and potential of a powerful voluntary organisation was
recognised by the Board of Control, set up to oversee the operation
of the Mental Deficiency Act 1913. Thomson describes how two
leading lights of the National Association for the Care and Control
of the Feeble-Minded, Mary Dendy herself, and Ellen Pinsent from
Birmingham, were made commissioners of the Board of Control,
while the Board moved rapidly to aid the establishment of a new
body, the CAMW.[194] The CAMW's role was envisioned as providing
a cheap source of labour to implement the Act; and to provide services
which were beyond the Act's remit – such as Occupation Centres,
after care committees, and 'friendly supervision' of borderline cases.
Despite the fact that the philosophy of the CAMW was pro-institutional
care, its role was limited to providing for care outside of institutions.
Thomson argues that it tacitly ceded institutional care to the statutory
sector (though there were many institutions, large and small, which
continued to be run by voluntary organisations) in return for a
quasi-official remit for community care. It was also useful in propounding
policies which were politically too sensitive for the statutory sector

to adopt, for example campaigns to prohibit marriage in the 1920s and for voluntary sterilisation in the 1930s. The relationship was a cosy symbiotic one – there was little perceptible difference in philosophy between the Board of Control and the CAMW, although increasingly a preference for paid professionals over volunteers on the part of Local Authorities, and within the CAMW itself, began to undermine the role of the CAMW as the 1930s went on.

The CAMW's role as an arm of the state, its developing profession-alisation, and indeed the seeds of its decline, are well illustrated in this example from Northamptonshire. In October 1932 the Board of Control wrote a stern letter to the Clerk to the Northamptonshire Mental Deficiency Committee saying that 'the general organisation of the Mental Deficiency service cannot be regarded as satisfactory'.[195]

In January 1933 the CAMW followed this up by offering the services of Miss Laxton, a CAMW organiser, to set up a local branch to run the service, at a cost of £240 per annum plus expenses. The Committee agreed to ask Miss Laxton to undertake a survey of the county's service in March. Miss Laxton's findings were an indict-ment of the status quo – only 90 people were under the care of the Committee; there should have been around 2,200 defectives in the county (extrapolating from national ascertainment rates), but only around 1,000 were known; the only resort was the institution; and only health visitors undertook supervisory visits. There is a distinct eugenic tone to the Report, which played on fears of defective children escaping detection and going on to reproduce yet more of their kind. The Report, presented to the Committee in November, recommended setting up a county wide branch of the CAMW, grant-aided by the County Council. However, although the Report did prompt the Mental Deficiency Committee to act, their decision was against a Voluntary Association. Instead, they decided to advertise for a salaried Mental Deficiency Officer – a post for which Miss Laxton applied unsuccessfully. This encapsulated neatly both the flavour of CAMW activity on behalf of the government, and its weakness, as Local Authorities could see little benefit in paying a voluntary organisation to provide services. Why choose what might be a critical and hard-to-manage voluntary organisation when for around the same cost a servant of the Local Authority could do the job?

The NAPBC had no such official status in its early days, and had to struggle for recognition. For example, in 1952 the local branch in Buckinghamshire wrote to the Buckinghamshire Mental Health Sub-Committee (successor to the Mental Deficiency Committee) requesting representation on a sub-committee which was considering the rebuilding of the Slough Occupation Centre after the Local Authority had decided to run it directly rather than through the Buckinghamshire Branch of the CAMW. The Committee replied that this was a statutory facility, therefore it was not appropriate for the organisation to have representation.[196] However, by 1955, when the NAPBC had 167 local branches, it was recognised to the extent that its members were invited to give evidence to the Royal Commission on the review of the Mental Deficiency and Lunacy Acts.

Influencing policy

Both organisations took steps to influence policy. The CAMW took a proactive role in areas such as encouraging training for staff in Occupation and Industrial Centres, and running courses, extending 'friendly supervision' to 'borderline cases', and encouraging Local Authorities to take a more energetic role in the implementation of the Mental Deficiency Acts (as in the example from Northamptonshire above). It had its own journal, *Mental Welfare*, which sought to inform a wider public about salient issues. Indeed, its secretary, Evelyn Fox, propounded one of the most coherent visions of community care in the inter-war years in the pages of the journal:

> *Community care should vary from the giving of purely friendly advice and help to the various forms of state guardianship with compulsory powers .... It should include the power of affording every kind of assistance to the defective – boarding out, maintenance grants, the provision of tools, travelling expenses to and from work, of temporary care, of change of air – in a word all those things which would enable a defective to remain safely in his family.*[197]

Although such visions were rarely if ever implemented in full, the CAMW's contribution was important in community care, an area of policy which was severely under-developed. But to the CAMW, community care was always second best to institutional care.

The NAPBC also attempted to influence policy, though its lack of official status initially impeded this. In their evidence to the 1954 Royal Commission, however, parents were able to draw attention to the unfairness of the term 'ineducable', the waiting lists of 25,000 children for places in Special Schools or Occupation Centres, the likelihood that in the absence of community provision people would need institutional care, the need for Health Visitors to have specific training in mental handicap, and career opportunities in the field for teachers and staff of Local Authority Children's Departments as well as nurses. The NAPBC argued that provision for children and families would mean fewer needing institutional care – its clear agenda was for more community care. Although none of these issues was satisfactorily addressed in the subsequent legislation, the 1959 Mental Health Act, it represents an agenda that has gradually infiltrated policy and practice – for example the 1971 Education Act did make it a statutory duty to educate all children, while subsequent Government policy documents, such as *Better Services for the Mentally Handicapped* (1971) espoused community care, and this remains officially the Government's position.

Publications and research were also pioneered by the NAPBC. One of its earliest manifestations was a newsletter edited by Judy Fryd, later to become *Parents' Voice*. Research activity was fostered by a research fund 'to support research into causation and prevention, treatment and remedial care, education and training' (1955).[198] It attracted some major names in the research field. The research sub-committee was chaired by Sir Cyril Burt, and a journal was founded, *The Journal of Mental Deficiency*. In the research field its influence on the development of 'family style' services is notable. One of its best known research efforts was the Brooklands experiment under the direction of Jack Tizard. This experiment monitored the results of moving a group of 16 children out of the Fountain Hospital, Tooting, to a private house, 'Brooklands', where they were 'cared for in small family groups'[199] under staff whose role was multi-disciplinary in terms of nursing, education and physical care. Later influential work sponsored by the Society included the Slough experiment, comprising 'family style' hostel care under a house mother and father, a model which took root from the late 1960s.

In its public image the NAPBC drew far less on the eugenic fears which the CAMW promulgated. Instead there emerged 'Little Stephen', the pathetic child who remained the Society's logo into the 1990s. This was both cause and effect of a change in public attitudes to mental handicap. No longer confined to the ghetto of the underclass – because so many members were very obviously respectable middle-class people – the NAPBC was part and parcel of the shift from seeing 'mental defect' as a hereditary taint associated with crime, immorality and disease to seeing it as a tragedy which could befall any parent, its members as unfortunate people 'burdened' with a never ending cycle of care, and properly deserving of publicly funded help.

Figure 14 - 'Little Stephen',
the logo of Mencap until the 1990s

At the local level

The CAMW

It was at the local level that the CAMW made its presence felt to 'defectives' and their families. In some areas there was already an extensive network of members when the 1913 Mental Deficiency Act passed into law. In Buckinghamshire, whose branch was founded in 1914, almost immediately the 1913 Act was implemented, there was an impressive network of local visitors covering nearly every parish. Visitors were overwhelmingly female, with the exception of a handful of vicars. The names include some honourables and peers, for example Lady Leon was the Visitor in Fenny Stratford, as well as being one of four Divisional secretaries.[200] In other Local Authorities, the branch was founded with encouragement from the CAMW, and was from the start a semi-professional organisation[201]; and in yet others, like Northamptonshire, no branch was ever founded.

Where local branches of the CAMW existed they had varying degrees of influence and activity, falling into broad spheres – ascertainment, visiting people under statutory supervision, service provision and lobbying for more state provision. These will be examined in turn, using examples drawn from three Local Authorities, Buckinghamshire, Bedfordshire and Somerset.

Ascertainment

Ascertainment was the job of actually locating suspected defectives and reporting them to the Local Authority Mental Deficiency Committee for medical examination and possible certification as mental defectives. In Buckinghamshire, the zeal of Visitors in seeking out possible defectives regularly overestimated its incidence. In 1923–4, 74 new cases were reported. Of these, only 42 were formally certified; similarly in 1924–5, 71 were ascertained, 41 certified. The arguments for local volunteers to be the means by which ordinary people crossed the boundary into becoming 'mental defectives' were put by Lord Onslow, Chair of the Buckinghamshire Association for the Care of the Feeble-Minded (it refused to change its name despite being prompted from the Centre), in 1924:

> *The members who lived in the vicinity of mental defectives were able to exercise tact and diplomacy and it was far better that neighbours, who were well known to be philanthropically disposed, should make the preliminary investigations.*[202]

However, the enthusiasm of the Visitors for new cases, although in line with national CAMW policy of encouraging 'friendly supervision' for 'borderline cases', may not have been so welcome to the beneficiaries. Local Authority officials often commented that the problems reported were 'much exaggerated'. The Voluntary Association instituted supervision prior to the full medical examination for certification, so any stigma would have lingered, even though the doctors decided against formal certification. It did have the effect, however, of giving impetus to lobbying for more facilities. At the 1925 AGM, Mrs Knapp, member of the Executive Committee, reported that they had 351 defectives under supervision: not all were suitable for institutional care, she argued, 'but we have taken away their liberty for their own good, however, it was necessary to give them a certain amount of instruction and comfort in place of that liberty'.[203]

The impact of an active local branch on ascertainment rates was considerable. In the same year (1925) that 351 cases of supervision were reported in Buckinghamshire there were 930 in Somerset, another county with an active branch, but only 17 in Bedfordshire where, as will be described below, the activity was confined to one quasi professional.

Statutory Supervision
It was in the role of supervising people in their homes that volunteers of the CAMW branches crossed the boundary from public to private in the most conspicuous way. Examples for this section are taken from Bedfordshire. In contrast to Buckinghamshire and Somerset, the Bedfordshire Local Association was not a grass roots organisation which had developed organically from pre-existing branches of the National Association for the Care and Control of the Feeble-Minded and allied organisations. The Bedfordshire Local Association was founded in the early 1920s, following pressure from the CAMW on the Local Authority to provide more than institutional care. The Local Association was closely bound up with the Bedford Rescue Home whose matrons, Miss Cariss, and later Miss Mumford, each became the secretary and who were paid an annual sum (£70 in the early 1930s) to visit defectives under supervision. Both appear to have carried out their duties conscientiously, filing quarterly reports to the clerk to the Mental Deficiency Committee on all the people under their 'care'. In 1925 there were 11 cases, and the Report focuses on their health, well being, general conduct, and daytime occupation. In the majority of cases the tone is benign, but behind the 'friendly' style lay the inevitable care-control dilemma of most welfare work – the threat of statutory intervention. Indeed, Visitors were expressly charged with ensuring that 'defectives' did not form relationships with the opposite sex.[204]

In Miss Cariss's case, the Rescue Home link with the cause of 'fallen girls' appears to have influenced her practice. She was assiduous, indeed zealous, in harrying the Mental Deficiency Committee to deal firmly with young women who, in her opinion, were in 'moral danger'. The Mental Deficiency Committee, as with ascertainment, tended to take a less urgent stance. Sarah G. was one object of Miss C.'s attentions. A former resident of the Bedford Rescue Home, she had been put on 'probation' (licence) in the household of the vicar of a country parish, and the possibility of discharging her altogether from the Acts was under consideration. Miss C. reported to the Mental Deficiency Committee in October 1925:

> *This girl ... has recently made the acquaintance of a youth. In spite of repeated warnings continues to meet him. She is with an exceptionally kind mistress and it will be a pity if she has to leave. It seems quite impossible to give any freedom without the fear of its being abused.*

The dispute between Miss Cariss and the Mental Deficiency Committee continued for some months over the period 1925–6. Eventually it transpired that Sarah was pregnant, and she was returned to the Bedford Poor Law Institution at the behest of the Board of Control.[205]

Visitors regularly crossed the boundaries between the statutory authorities, the families and 'defectives' they visited, and the Board of Control. The latter could be drawn in, as in Sarah G's case, to insist upon action. It was the Visitors who actually entered people's homes, and their opinions could influence the long-term fates of their supervisees, but there were many complex negotiations along the way. In the case of George C., for example, the Visitor decided in 1935 that he would be better off in an institution, 'as there is no mother, and the lad is left all day without supervision'. Over the following year she managed to persuade George's father that the 'training' on offer in Bromham Hospital would be good for him, and George duly went there in 1936.[206]

Service provision
Where Voluntary Organisations were strong, they rapidly took on service-providing roles. Somerset was one of the Board of Control's star performers, appearing high in its 'league tables' for rates of ascertainment, certification and institutional provision.[207] As early as 1920 the Association was considering a scheme for the establishment of Occupation Centres, and by 1929 five were in place. The Occupation Centres were seen as 'one of the most satisfactory means of keeping in touch with defectives living in their own homes or under guardianship',[208] i.e. they were seen as a means of exercising more effective control over non-institutionalised defectives.

In Buckinghamshire, too, the Voluntary Organisation ran Occupation Centres – the one in Slough opened in the 1930s and was only taken under direct Local Authority Control in 1952. Other efforts were directed at locating suitable guardians – an advert was placed in parish magazines in 1926; visiting Poor Law Institutions licensed to take mental defectives and running classes for inmates; providing home tutors for children and supplying after care to people after they were discharged.

Large-scale service providing activities like Occupation Centres were financed by Local Authority grants,[209] but a great deal of the day-to-day work was done by unpaid female volunteers.

It is in its lobbying activities that the ethos of the CAMW is most clearly discernible. As Thomson notes, the CAMW always saw community care as second best to institutional care, and, given that community care was its sphere of influence, its arguments tended to undermine its role. There was a constant flow of appeals at Annual General Meetings for more facilities, particularly for institutions, but also, in Buckinghamshire, for special school classes. These appeals drew upon ascertainment and certification statistics. The CAMW generally, and some local branches, was also active in promoting further measures to restrict the sexual activities of people with learning difficulties. The CAMW joined the campaign for voluntary sterilisation in the 1930s,[210] and local branches flirted with various other schemes for regulation of sexual activity. The Somerset Association recommended in 1927 that legislation be introduced to prevent 'the marriage of the unfit',[211] and Mrs Hodgson of the Eugenics Society addressed the 1924 AGM of the Buckinghamshire Association in favour of marriage regulation.

Overall, although it might be plausibly argued that the work of local branches of the CAMW did benefit some people, in the provision of Occupation Centres and in offering a helping hand to some of those under supervision, its overall policy was for more institutional care and more legislation to curb the rights of 'mental defectives'. A eugenic undertone is discernible in many of its public pronouncements – it did little or nothing to counter the stigma attached to the subjects of its attentions.

The NAPBC at the local level

The NAPBC's local activity was, like that of the CAMW, patchy and variable. The number of branches grew very rapidly in the first ten years. The first were formed in Ipswich, Cambridge and Torquay in 1947–8 and by 1956 there were 200 branches with 12,000 members.[212] Unlike the CAMW membership of local worthies, members of NAPBC Local Societies were motivated by their own plight. One early member recalls the impetus to her founding a local branch as the pronouncement of her son's ineducability, and the despair consequent on finding there were no places for him to go. She was inspired by attending a meeting at which Judy Fryd spoke:

> *Yes, yes, she was the founder of the movement. Wonderful woman. I was absolutely inspired by her. I was so moved because she said everything that was on my mind. Until I read her article, '40,000 lame chicks' in the Sunday People the only other person that I knew was Mr and Mrs R. who were friendly with my sister in law. They had a Down's boy, Alan. I didn't know it happened to anyone else.*[213]

Similarly, Jean Morton, a founder member of Derby Mencap recalled:

> *Derby Mencap started in 1956 because there was nothing for handicapped children. In those days, they [families] had to bring them up themselves.*[214]

Actually discovering families with 'backward' children was an issue in the early days. Rene Harris, one of the founder members of the Luton Society (founded 1955)[215] recalled, in an oral history interview conducted in 1991, that the Society had difficulty in identifying its potential membership:

> *This lady (Mental Welfare Officer) helped me found the Society really because she couldn't reveal any names, so we wrote invitations to a party and gave them to her and she passed them onto people. I'll never forget that first party because I didn't know anything about mentally handicapped people except my own, no idea how to cope with them – but I was very good at catering.*

In terms of providing services, many local branches undertook to fund-raise to fill in gaps. As the focus was initially on children, these services tended to be child-oriented. The first service to be organised nationally was Orchard Dene, at Rainhill, financed by public donations following 'Good Cause' broadcasts which raised £1,000. Orchard Dene, opened in March 1952, was a short stay respite home, for children whose families were in crisis. As respite care was only beginning to be developed by Local Authorities in the early 1950s, this is typical of the type of gap-filling that NAPBC focussed on. Other types of provision, sponsored and run by Local Societies, included nursery classes for very young children, run by volunteers, holidays and outings, and leisure clubs, forerunners of the Gateway Clubs now such a feature of local Mencap activity. The Luton 'Wednesday Club' was founded in the 1950s.

Funding was essentially through charitable donations, and money-raising activities – bazaars, sale of Christmas cards, and sponsorship from local firms. The car firm, Vauxhall, organised an annual pram race for its apprentices to raise money for the Luton Society.

Of course, lobbying for more state-funded provision was central to NAPBC, both locally and nationally. The fear of having to take the advice she had been given, to 'put him away and forget about him' was, according to Rene Harris, a great motivating factor, 'Throughout the 1950s and early 1960s the one fear of my parents was that their child would have to go to Bromham'. Through newsletters and Annual Reports, Local Societies informed their members of what might be possible, drawing on NAPBC research like the Brooklands and Slough experiments which showed the advantages of 'family style' services – and this translated into pressure locally to take action, initially for children, but, as the children of the original membership grew up, for adults too. The maturing of the Society in the early 1960s coincided with the great expansion of Day Centres (successors to Occupation Centres) and the founding of many Local Authority Hostels, all of which were eagerly anticipated, and to a greater or lesser extent steered, by members of the NAPBC and its successor organisations.

In terms of the public – private boundary which voluntary organisations straddle, the CAMW appears through its local activities to represent an extension of the public into the private world of the family with a member with a learning disability, while the members of the NAPBC used it as a means by which they could move out from their private domain and represent their issues in the public world.

Conclusion

In this chapter I have argued that the early 1950s was an important boundary-crossing period in the history of learning disability. Prior to that, while the CAMW was the dominant voluntary organisation in the field, mental deficiency was a matter of shame. Public attitudes were such that people hid the fact that they had a child with an intellectual disability as far as they could. The CAMW, although it did a great deal to ameliorate the position in some areas by providing community care services, did nothing to challenge the dominant view that society was best served by putting people in institutions. Its public pronouncements were part and parcel of the eugenic agenda.

The foundation of the NAPBC is both symbol and cause of shifting perceptions. Parent members from that time speak of moving from darkness into light, as they discovered that, not only were they not alone, they also had a just cause to demand a better deal for themselves and their children. The image of people with learning disabilities changed from 'danger' to 'innocent' as respectable middle-class parents, even well known celebrities like Brian Rix, went public and demanded recognition and change. It is now clear that this agenda too is shifting under the influence of rights discourses such as self-advocacy – but that is a chapter in its own right.

This examination of the specifics of the situation in learning disability modifies the picture of the role of voluntary organisations presented by Jane Lewis and others. It shows a distinct change in the role of voluntary organisations, at least in learning disability around mid century, from being an extension of the state apparatus, with a similar philosophy, to developing an advocacy role for parents. This in its turn contributed to changing public perceptions of the people the NAPBC spoke for; no longer primarily working-class objects of suspicion, but respectable, often middle-class people, 'burdened with care', deserving of more sympathy and support.

[175] This was called the Central Association for the Care of Mental Defectives until 1921. See M. Thomson *The 'Problem' of Mental Deficiency in England and Wales 1913-1946*, (Clarendon Press: Oxford, 1998). Like Thomson, I refer to the organisation throughout as the CAMW for simplicity. Thomson's chapter 'The Community Care Solution' is a masterly account of the role of the CAMW from a national perspective, and I have drawn heavily on it in writing this.

[176] Founded in 1946. Although Mencap is a much more familiar name, the abbreviation NAPBC is used throughout this chapter because it is historically more accurate.

[177] Although the NAPBC temporarily was housed in the premises of the CAMW in the early 1950s, the two organisations were not formally connected.

[178] Beds. CRO *Report of County Medical Officer to Mental Deficiency Committee,* January 1949.

[179] Beds. CRO *Report of Visitors to Turvey Occupation Centre to Mental Health Sub Committee,* 1951.

[180] J. W. Trent, *Inventing the Feeble Mind: A History of Mental Retardation in the United States*, (University of California Press, 1994), p.230.

[181] Jane Lewis, 'Gender, the family and women's agency in the building of welfare states: the British case', *Social History*, 19 (1) (1994); Anthea Symonds and Ann Kelly (eds), *The Social Construction of Community Care*, (London, 1997).

[182] Jane Lewis, *The Voluntary Sector, the State and Social Work in Britain*, (Aldershot, 1995), p.3.

[183] Pat Thane, *The Foundations of the Welfare State (second edition)*, (Harlow, 1990), p.1.

[184] G. Finlayson, 'A Moving Frontier: Voluntarism and the State in British Social Welfare 1911-1949', *Twentieth Century British History,* 1, (1990), 183-206.

[185] Lewis, *The Voluntary Sector*, p. 9.

[186] Lewis, Ibid., p.16.

[187] Lewis, *'Gender, the family'*, p.39.

[188] Greta Jones, *Social Hygiene in Twentieth Century Britain*, (London: Croom Helm, 1986); Mark Jackson, 'Institutional Provision for the Feeble Minded in Edwardian England' in, Wright, D. and Digby, A. (eds), *From Idiocy to Mental Deficiency: Historical Perspectives on People with Learning Disabilities* (London: Routledge, 1996).

[189] Jackson , 'Institutional provision'.

[190] Jones, *Social Hygiene*, pp.53-4.

[191] Victoria Shennan, *Our Concern: The Story of the National Association for Mentally Handicapped Children and Adults,* (London: National Association for Mentally Handicapped Children and Adults, 1980).

[192] Shennan, *Our Concern*, p.10.

[193] Shennan, Ibid., p.13.

[194] Thomson, *Problem of Mental Deficiency*, Chapter 4.

[195] Northants. CRO, Letter from Board of Control to Clerk to the Northamptonshire Mental Deficiency Committee, October 1932.

[196] Bucks. CRO *Minutes of the Mental Health Sub Committee*, February 1952.

[197] Evelyn Fox, 'Community Schemes for the Social Control of Mental Defectives', Mental Welfare 11 (3), (1930), p.71.

[198] Shennan, *Our Concern*, p.13.

[199] Shennan, Ibid., p.16.

[200] See also D. Atkinson, 'Learning from Local History: Evidence from Somerset', in Atkinson, D., Jackson, M. and Walmsley, J. (eds.), *Forgotten Lives: Discovering the History of Learning Disability,* (Kidderminster: BILD Publications, 1997). This shows a strong grass roots organisation existing pre 1913.

[201] Bedfordshire was one such - see below.

[202] Bucks. VAMD Minutes Vol. 2 Report of Annual General Meeting 1924.

[203] Bucks. VAMD Minutes Vol. 2 Report of Annual General Meeting 1925.

[204] For more detail see J. Walmsley, 'Uncovering community care', in Atkinson, Jackson, and Walmsley, *Forgotten Lives.*

[205] Beds. CRO Mental Deficiency Papers Vol. 9 passim.

[206] Beds. CRO Mental Deficiency Papers Vol. 23.

[207] D. Atkinson, 'Learning from Local History: Evidence from Somerset', in Atkinson, Jackson and Walmsley, *Forgotten Lives.*

[208] Ruth Darwin, 'The Proper Control of Defectives Outside Institutions'. Paper given at the 1926 Conference on Mental Welfare, Taunton.

[209] For details see Thomson, *Problem of Mental Deficiency,* Chapter 4.

[210] Thomson, *Problem of Mental Deficiency*, pp.142-3.

[211] Quoted in J. Walmsley, D. Atkinson, and S. Rolph, 'Community Care and Mental Deficiency', in Bartlett, P. and Wright, D. (eds), *Outside the Walls of the Asylum*, (London: Athlone, 1999).

[212] Shennan, *Our Concern*, p.9.

[213] Oral History Interview with author, June 1991 - the speaker wished to remain anonymous.

[214] Quoted in *Learning Disability: Working as Equal People,* Workbook 2 from Open University pack, (Milton Keynes: Open University Press, 1996), p.84.

Chapter 9

Ambiguous boundaries: retrieving the history of learning disability nursing

Duncan Mitchell

Summary

In this chapter, Duncan Mitchell discusses the extent to which there can be a shared history between people with learning difficulties and those who work with them. He considers the similarities and differences between groups of people sharing the same institutional space, and often doing similar work, within the colonies and institutions built for people with learning difficulties in the twentieth century. In addition, he explores the effects of nursing on people with learning difficulties and the relationship between learning disability nursing and the rest of the nursing profession. Nurses were part of an oppressive system of control within institutions in which they maintained considerable power over people with learning difficulties, who were generally denied citizenship.[216] Nevertheless, nurses and people with learning difficulties shared the same institutional space, often performed similar work, and have both been relegated to the margins of history. The aim of this chapter is to retrieve their history by focusing on the boundaries between people with learning difficulties and their nurses, and between learning disability nurses and the rest of the nursing profession. Duncan illustrates that, although boundaries existed between people with learning difficulties and their paid carers, the boundaries were, in some instances, ambiguous. He shows how examining their histories jointly can give deeper insights into the past.

Introduction

Caring for people with learning difficulties has had a number of guises since its formal adoption as nursing in 1917 by the Medico-Psychological Association (MPA) and by the General Nursing Council (GNC) in the early 1920s. Known originally as 'mental deficiency nursing', the name itself reflected and reinforced changes in fashion and policy direction: it became mental subnormality nursing after 1959, mental handicap nursing in the early 1980s and learning disability nursing in the early 1990s. Both the MPA and the GNC treated mental deficiency nursing as a separate part of mental nursing, demonstrating their uncertainty as to whether this infant part of the profession would expand and develop, or would wither away. Even in the 1940s the GNC was still questioning the need for such a separate branch of nursing.[217]

The early development of attendants and nurses within asylums has been well documented[218] but the implementation of the 1913 Mental Deficiency Act led to a need for a workforce within the mental deficiency institutions. This nursing workforce became a separate group within nursing and, although there were often mental and general nurses working in learning disability institutions, it was rarely a two-way process: nurses in learning disability were not usually permitted to work in establishments other than the colonies and institutions in which they were specifically trained to work. This unequal treatment has continued to be a central problem in the relationship between different parts of the profession. Compared to the rest of the nursing profession, learning disability nurses were a small group and, as far as the profession was concerned, remained an anomaly within an occupation that was striving for greater professional status.

The chapter is divided into four sections.[219] The first considers the nature of work within learning disability institutions and argues that people with learning difficulties undertook a range of tasks, including those associated with nursing care. I will suggest that there were no clear boundaries between the work of people with learning difficulties and that of employees of the institutions, other than the important one of pay. The second section examines the place of the nurse within learning disability institutions, and asks why the nursing profession became so involved in what was essentially a social rather than a health service. The third section considers the effects that the presence of nurses had on people with learning difficulties and suggests that nursing contributed to the medicalisation of the service. Finally, I will examine the relationship between learning disability nursing and the rest of the nursing profession. I will suggest that learning disability nurses were marginalised within the profession because of their inability to conform to the image of nursing as a sickness-based profession.

The nature of work within learning disability institutions

Institutions for people with learning difficulties were complex organisations and in order to function they required many different types of work. People with learning difficulties participated in all institutional activities with the exception of medical care. The work they carried out was vital to the running of the institutions but was largely unpaid. The activities which were carried out ranged from the repetitive and mundane to the varied and complex. This suited the needs of those who ran the institutions rather than the people who lived in them and is illustrated by the following passage written by the medical superintendent of the Royal Eastern Counties Asylum, who argued for mixed institutions:

> *The all-grade institution is more economical. The high grades do the skilled work for the low grades, the low grades do the unskilled work for the higher grades. An institution composed of high grade cases alone would be very nice, but there would be a very great waste of labour. Much of their time would be taken up in doing work that might easily be done by lower grade patients ... Those who can do housework even though not very high grade, can do the housework of that part of the Institution where there will be helpless idiot cases who can do nothing for themselves. The nursery can find useful employment for some of the higher grade women helping under supervision to look after the children.*[220]

This demonstrates the variety of work undertaken and the importance to the institution of that work. It also suggests that it did not stop at the support work of cleaning and catering, or the agricultural and industrial tasks, but involved care work. Residents of the institutions looked after other, less able, residents as part of their individual work. Turner refers to the nursery where 'high grade' women could look after children, under supervision. However, the care of residents by other residents appears to have been far more widespread with paid nurses taking on a supervisory role. A Board of Control file in the Public Records Office contains requests from learning disability institutions for residents to do either fully paid work, work with pocket money, or to lose their 'mental defective' status and work as members of staff.[221] A small number of people who had been classified as 'mental defectives' went on to become probationer nurses. The only concern of the Board of Control was that they did not continue to care for people with whom they had shared the status of patient.[222] Thomson argues that 'lower grade' patients were under the sole supervision of 'higher grades' as late as 1951. 'This practice was not confined to mental deficiency institutions: defectives were also valued as supplementary staff in public assistance institutions and mental hospitals, so much so that transfer to mental deficiency colonies was often resisted.'[223] My own experience of paid work in a large institution in Lancashire bears this out in that many elderly women talked fondly of 'their low grades' referring to the young people they had looked after in the past. Their description of the work that they carried out involved total care either of one person or of a group of young people.

There were also some highly responsible and complex tasks carried out by some residents of the institutions. One retired nurse of a Yorkshire institution tells of a resident of the institution who worked in the office and was responsible for drawing up staff rotas and annual leave arrangements for the entire nursing staff of the institution.[224] In addition to the work inside the institutions, residents also supported the institutions by working outside them and earning money which helped pay for their 'care'. The medical superintendent of Turner Village in Colchester, writing about a mental deficiency colony during the Second World War, notes that 'medium and high grade' girls earned £30 in currant-picking outside the institution during the fruit-picking season and £28 of this was credited to the local authorities who were responsible for funding the girls.[225]

The position in learning disability institutions, therefore, was not simply one of a paid group of workers being responsible for a group of people resident in the institution. The work that was carried out was done by a variety of people, both paid and unpaid. Many people with learning difficulties carried out the work that is more usually associated with nurses. It could be argued that many were nurses insofar as the work they carried out involved the direct care of other people. There were often no clear boundaries between people with learning difficulties and paid employees of the institutions in terms of the work performed. There needs to be recognition of the contribution that people with learning difficulties have made, not only to their own care but to the care and economic support of others.

The clear difference between people with learning difficulties and their paid carers was that of power. Learning disability nursing was near the bottom end of a paid hospital hierarchy,[226] but individual nurses often had considerable control over their own areas of work and significant power over the people with learning difficulties within those areas. Any power exercised by people with learning difficulties was always tempered by their restriction to the institution and by the possibility of withdrawal of privileges.

Why did nurses become the dominant group within the institutions?

Although it is clear that many residents of the institutions contributed to a large extent to the work that was needed to run them, there was never a suggestion that people with learning difficulties might organise themselves within their institutions. The emphasis of the Mental Deficiency Act was that people defined as being mentally deficient needed care and control. They might well have been able to provide their own care but were perceived to need people to control them. This task fell to nurses under the direction, at least in many institutions, of doctors. The development of nursing within mental deficiency institutions tends to be understood in terms of the medicalisation of mental deficiency allied with the development of mental health nursing. Although this is clearly an important factor, it tends to overlook the tensions and ambiguities in slotting the broader, more social model of care, which was carried out within the mental deficiency institutions, into a narrower sickness/health model of nursing.

One crucial factor in the development of specific nursing for people with learning difficulties can be related to periodisation. At the same time as the implementation of the 1913 Mental Deficiency Act, legislation regulating the nursing profession was passed. This helped to change the way that nursing as a term, and as an occupation, was understood. 'Nursing' gradually ceased to be a term for any caring work that was undertaken by women, and began to assume a specifically defined sickness role. Prior to the statutory regulation of nursing, the term nurse was largely gender specific and involved all women involved in care. Florence Nightingale went so far as to say that at some time 'every woman is a nurse' because at one time or another the majority of women had been responsible for the personal health of another person.[227] The campaign, mainly by hospital nurses, to formally regulate the profession was not intended to include mental nurses, let alone a totally new group of mental deficiency nurses. The campaigners intended to support the professionalisation of hospital-trained sickness nurses. The inclusion of mental nurses and the creation of learning disability nurses as a formal group was not the intention of many of the campaigners. Nolan makes this clear when he points out the antipathy to mental nurses of Mrs Bedford Fenwick, one of the leading campaigners for state registration, and the general animosity from the nursing establishment.[228]

The origins of paid care for people with learning difficulties are difficult to discern. There is very little evidence upon which to build because of the sparse amount written about those who worked with people with learning difficulties. Andrews suggests that workers with people with learning difficulties are part of a hidden history. When writing about provision for the mentally disabled in early modern London he claims that those who cared for the 'simple minded' are just as neglected as those who were cared for.[229] Andrews explains that it was usually the parish nurse who looked after a variety of cases including the learning disabled; this sometimes involved a degree of specialisation. Men did get involved but tended only to be concerned with the more troublesome cases; moreover they were paid more. Rushton argues that by the eighteenth century:

> *There was a limited growth of acknowledged expertise in dealing with awkward individuals which, though it did not amount to the equivalent of a modern profession, was nevertheless essential to local communities. While, therefore, there were no real 'experts' in mental disabilities before the*

eighteenth century asylums, there were many constables, gaolers and keepers of workhouses and houses of correction who were trusted to deal with the persons allocated to them. In villages and families, too, there may have been those with accepted skills.[230]

In the latter part of the nineteenth, and early twentieth, century, workhouses which segregated people with learning difficulties in separate wards or blocks employed people termed 'imbecile nurses' or 'epileptic nurses'. There is no evidence to suggest that these people were seen in any way as specialists but they certainly had separate areas of work to other staff. A history of work with people with learning difficulties, prior to the twentieth century, has yet to be constructed in a similar way to the history of nursing prior to formal institutional nursing.[231] What is important is that those women who did the work were popularly called nurses and that their work with people with learning difficulties was seen as part and parcel of their duties as nurses.

When the 1913 Mental Deficiency Act was implemented it may have seemed natural to refer to women workers as 'nurses'. However, the MPA was looking for a strong toehold within institutions and one way to do this was to control training and promote the use of nurses. The Board of Control was also intent on ensuring that a trained workforce staffed the institutions in order to attract suitable employees and to promote standards. Nursing was the most obvious professional group to promote because of its history of working in asylums and because its organisation was new and pliable.

The effects of nursing on people with learning difficulties

On the immediate human level, the effect of the presence of nurses on people with learning difficulties was mixed and depended as much on the individuals concerned as on the existing hierarchy. As in any other professional or occupational group, some individuals were kind and others unkind, while some were a mixture of both. The system of control that existed clearly encouraged those who had a controlling nature.[232] Accounts by people with learning difficulties differ considerably in their descriptions of staff but what is clear is the significant influence staff could have on their day to day lives.[233]

However, what was perhaps more important than individual relationships, which would have been variable whatever the occupational group, was the way people with learning difficulties became defined as 'sick'. In this respect, nursing has been part of the medicalisation of services. If people assume that they need nurses only if they are ill, people with learning difficulties who need nurses will be seen as ill. The association between nursing and illness has almost certainly contributed to a negative view of people with learning difficulties as 'sick', especially as images of nursing have become increasingly associated with images of illness.

Wolfensberger's analysis of the way human services are valued, or devalued, is useful in understanding the effect of nursing on the image of people with learning difficulties.[234] Wolfensberger argues that it is an underlying belief in deviance that translates itself into human services, thus creating a vicious circle. In twentieth-century Britain, the two prevailing and coexisting views of people with learning difficulties have been as a menace to society, so creating institutions to contain them, and of diseased organisms, leading to the creation of hospitals with doctors and nurses to care for them. The latter process, of medicalisation, is pertinent and it has been argued that people with learning difficulties have been under the control of the medical profession, supported by nurses, for much of the century. However, it is important not to over-simplify the medicalisation perspective. Thomson points out the low esteem in which the medical specialists in mental deficiency were held by the rest of the profession, and the fact that, before the Second World War, most institutions remained under non-medical management.[235] In the period before the Second World War learning disability nursing contributed to the medicalisation of learning disability only in name, as the term nursing became more associated with caring for the sick. The work itself was essentially social and supervisory. The frequent complaints by members of the GNC, that there was not enough sickness or bed-side nursing in mental deficiency institutions to justify the training, bear this out.[236]

It was not until after the Second World War, when colonies and institutions were taken over by the National Health Service (NHS) and the GNC took full control of nurse training from the RMPA, that learning disability nursing began to be forced along the sickness route. It has been argued that it was the NHS that set the seal on the medicalisation of institutional learning disability services by the manner in which it 'almost incidentally, turned colonies into hospitals, local authority doctors into medical superintendents and consultants, and attendants into nurses.'[237]

Relationship between general nursing and learning disability nursing

Learning disability nursing has had an uncomfortable relationship with the general nursing profession. Learning disability nursing has never been fully accepted as nursing by the nursing hierarchy, but at the same time it has never been formally rejected. Nursing, under the umbrella of the GNC, has tried to project an image and a practice of learning disability nursing that has been alien to the nature of its work. At points throughout its history, the GNC has tried to ensure that learning disability nursing has been dominated by ideas of sickness and bedside nursing. It has been critical of those elements of learning disability nursing that did not conform to that image. At the same time, it has recognised that it was unlikely to be able to remove learning disability nursing from the profession because of pressure from both the MPA and the Board of Control. It sought to institutionalise its difference to learning disability nursing by defining 'real' or 'proper nursing' and by making it clear that learning disability nursing was something else. There were similarities to the relationship between the GNC and mental nursing but the key difference was that mental nurses were able to assume a sickness mantle because they dealt with the mentally ill.

In response to the anomaly, the GNC tried to isolate the acceptable nursing elements of learning disability nursing from those that involved containment, training, or education. This can be most easily identified in the language used to describe learning disability nurses. References to 'people involved in the training and care', or 'the nursing and training' of people with learning difficulties, rather than the simple term 'nursing' which was used for all other branches of the profession, demonstrates a qualification to the term 'nurse'.[238] This process can also be seen in the reports of the GNC which clearly separated the work that learning disability nurses did into that which was acceptable in nursing terms and that which was defined as training, education, or control.[239] This led to a marginalisation of learning disability nursing within the profession of nursing. The

GNC Reports on individual institutions, from the 1940s onwards, are remarkable in that they make little mention of the important issues of lifestyles, activities, and surroundings of people with learning difficulties but concentrate almost entirely on the clinical and technical aspects of physical nursing care considered to be legitimate nursing tasks.

It is probable that the GNC's insistence on clinical nursing skills assisted in the medicalisation of learning disability. It certainly meant that paid workers within learning disability institutions were less likely to develop their own specialist skills as a result of the concentration on hospital nursing skills. It is also clear from the relationship between learning disability nursing and general nursing that learning disability nurses were at the bottom of a professional hierarchy. This had unfortunate consequences for the recruitment and retention of suitable people to work with people with learning difficulties. Throughout much of the century it has been notoriously difficult to recruit nurses but even more difficult to recruit learning disability nurses, as they meet the criteria to be defined as an undervalued group.[240]

Ambiguous boundaries

Is there such a thing as shared history? On the one hand there clearly is. Nurses and people with learning difficulties shared some of the same space, lived in the same institutions, and shared similar work. On the other hand there were considerable differences. When this paper was first presented, the suggestion that there might be a shared stigma between those who worked with people with learning difficulties within institutions and people with learning difficulties themselves was heavily criticised by people who objected to the comparison between oppressed and oppressor. This criticism is clearly valid. Nurses for people with learning difficulties were part of an oppressive system and, although they may have been at the bottom of a professional hierarchy, they were none-the-less part of the profession. People with learning difficulties were an oppressed group; at the very least their freedom was removed or under threat of removal. Nurses for people with learning difficulties were paid, had union protection, had the same degree of freedom as any working-class person and were able to move out of the occupation they undertook. People with learning difficulties were unpaid, had little protection and few freedoms and could not move out of the social group to which they had been assigned.

Nevertheless, both people with learning difficulties and their paid carers are part of a hidden history. If we are to understand the nature and cause of oppression, then the history of nurses must be retrieved in parallel with that of people with learning difficulties.

---

216 This issue is explored further by David Barron (see Chapter 2) and Maureen Oswin (see Chapter 10). For a fuller discussion of issues related to 'citizenship', see Tim Stainton (Chapter 7).

217 Minutes of meetings between the General Nursing Council (GNC) and the Medico Psychological Association (MPA), later the Royal Medico Psychological Association (RMPA), demonstrate the reluctance of the GNC to take learning disability nursing fully on board. Public Records Office, DT16/241.

218 See for example P. Nolan, *A History of Mental Health Nursing,* (London: Chapman and Hall, 1993).

219 The four main sections of the chapter broadly follow the sections given in a paper to the Social History of Learning Disability Research Group's conference, *Inclusion and Exclusion,* but have been substantially revised in the light of points raised in the discussion that followed the presentation.

220 F. D. Turner, 'Notes about institutions for defectives', *Studies in Mental Inefficiency*, 1, (1920), 32-38.

221 *Employment of Mental Defectives in Hospitals,* Public Records Office, MH51/457.

222 *Board of Control Minutes,* 13.2.34, *Employment of Mental Defectives in Hospitals,* Public Records Office, MH51/457.

223 M. Thomson, *The Problem of Mental Deficiency: Eugenics, Democracy and Social Policy in Britain c.1870-1959*, (Oxford: Clarenden Press, 1998), p.139.

224 In discussion with the author as part of a yet unpublished oral history project on learning disability nursing.

225 E. Benjacar, 'A mental deficiency institution in war time', *Mental Health*, 1, (1940), 107-112.

226 For an illustration of the complex hierarchical structure within one learning disability institution, see A. Stevens, 'Recording the history of an institution: the Royal Eastern Counties Institution at Colchester', in Atkinson, D., Jackson, M. and Walmsley, J. (eds), *Forgotten Lives: Exploring the History of Learning Disability,* (Kidderminster: BILD Publications, 1997), p.58.

[227] F. Nightingale, 'Notes on Nursing: what is it and what it is not', (first published 1859, Edinburgh: Churchill Livingstone).

[228] Nolan, *A History of Mental Health Nursing.*

[229] J. Andrews, 'Identifying and providing for the mentally disabled in early modern London', in Wright, D. and Digby, A. (eds), *From Idiocy to Mental Deficiency: Historical Perspectives on People with Learning Difficulties,* (London: Routledge, 1996), pp.65-92.

[230] P. Rushton, 'Idiocy, the family and community in early modern north east England', in Wright and Digby, *From Idiocy to Mental Deficiency,* pp.44-64.

[231] For an example of such histories of general nursing, see R. Dingwall, A. M. Rafferty and C. Webster, *An Introduction to the Social History of Nursing,* (London: Routledge, 1988), or more recently, A. M. Rafferty, *The Politics of Nursing Knowledge,* (London: Routledge, 1996).

[232] Both David Barron (see Chapter 2) and Maureen Oswin (see Chapter 10) write critical accounts of nurses and attendants within the institutions. Barron emphasises the controlling environment while Oswin stresses the self-interest that suppressed change and criticism.

[233] See for example, J. Deacon, *Tongue Tied,* (London: Mencap, 1974); M. Potts and R. Fido, *'A fit person to be removed': Personal Accounts of Life in a Mental Deficiency Institution,* (Plymouth: Northcote House, 1991); M. Cooper, 'Mabel Cooper's life story', in Atkinson, D., Jackson, M. and Walmsley, J. *Forgotten Lives: Exploring the History of Learning Disability,* Kidderminster: BILD Publications, 1997) pp.21-34.

[234] W. Wolfensberger, *The Principle of Normalisation in Human Services*, (Toronto: National Institute for Mental Retardation, 1972).

[235] Thomson, *The Problem of Mental Deficiency*, p.131.

[236] This is explored further in D. Mitchell, 'Learning disability nursing: reflections on history', *Journal of Learning Disabilities for Nursing, Health and Social Care,* 2, (1998), 45-49.

[237] J. Brown and I. Walton, *How Nurses Learn: A National Study of the Training of Nurses in Mental Handicap,* (University of York, 1984), p.2.

[238] These examples are from minutes of the GNC in the early 1920s, Public Records Office, DT5/1.

[239] Most institutions were regularly inspected by the GNC from after the Second World War, although a few had earlier inspections. The reports can be seen in the Public Records Office, DT35.

[240] The differences of recruitment into general nursing and learning disability nursing are explored further in D. Mitchell, 'Learning disability nursing in the post war period', *International History of Nursing Journal,* 1, (1996), 20-33.

Chapter 10

Revisiting 'The Empty Hours'

Maureen Oswin

Summary

In this account of working with children who had multiple disabilities and lived permanently in long-stay hospitals, Maureen Oswin describes how this particular group of children formed a sub-group of their own within the already isolated institutions. Other residents, as well as the staff, would label these children as 'low-grades'. They did not even have the meagre opportunities which might have been available to more able residents. Government, local authorities, trade unions, and some voluntary organisations believed that this group of children should be permanently institutionalised. However, they not only suffered immense emotional deprivation, but due to physical neglect they often became frail and deformed. To cross boundaries of prejudice, to campaign for these children and work to convince colleagues and other professionals that they were neglected, meant facing considerable professional disapproval.

I started working with children with disabilities in 1959, at Queen Mary's Hospital in Carshalton, Surrey. That is going back nearly forty years, so what I say may sound very old-fashioned.

At that time Queen Mary's was still partly a hospital for treating sick children. It had acres of lovely grounds and the buildings were all red-brick separate villas in the style of early twentieth-century tuberculosis hospitals. Each villa had four large wards built around a courtyard, plus a small staff room, an office, and a kitchen for making drinks and toast.

Due to advances in medical knowledge, and the prevention of tuberculosis and polio, there was a drop in the number of sick children using the hospital, so in the 1950s a growing number of children with chronic physical disabilities such as muscular dystrophy or cerebral palsy were housed in the spare villas.

I was assigned to teach in the Cerebral Palsy Unit. About twenty children lived there, aged from four to mid-teens, and some had a degree of learning disability as well as cerebral palsy. School took place in one big room, physiotherapy in another, the children ate and lived in the third room and slept altogether in the fourth. There was no privacy, not even in the lavatories.

When the physiotherapists and teachers went home the children had a strict hospital regime, going to bed at 5 p.m. and sometimes being got up as early as 4.30 am., in order to fit in with staff duty times. Their life-style was very abnormal. They never went out of the hospital. They were living out their childhood in just four large rooms, cared for by a variety of staff who were constantly changing. They were dressed in clothes which came from a shared clothing pool and looked like they were all made in the same cheap clothing factory – of a thick board-like woolly material, shapeless and hard-wearing. All the clothes had a large label sewn into the collar, saying Queen Mary's Hospital, and under the label would be the number of the villa. Sometimes clothes got mixed up in the laundry and a child would be put into a jumper which had the wrong villa number on it or even the name of another hospital in Surrey. In those days, Surrey abounded in institutions.

The children never saw food cooked, it all came to the villas from the Central Kitchen in metal containers stacked in little run-about trollies. The children had no idea that potatoes were once earthy and had brown skins, they did not know what growing cabbages looked like, or where butter came from; nor had they smelt the inside of a baker's shop or seen fancy cakes on display.

Occasionally, with the help of a physiotherapist, I pushed the children's wheelchairs to the Central Laundry, where the kindly laundry workers would welcome us at the door and we could stare at the giant washing machines turning over the institutional clothes. Or we would go and peep into the Central Kitchens and stare in amazement at huge slabs of cheese, mountains of cut white bread, long tables with staff frantically chopping up food and tipping it into giant boilers, and peeling hundreds of eggs.

Everything was on a large scale – monstrous laundries, monstrous kitchens, hefty bundles of shared clothing – nothing was child-sized and family-sized.

The children were lucky if they had a cuddle or if they had any staff who stayed long enough to really get to know them. They lived totally institutionalised lives, excluded from the rest of society.

During the mid-1960s many children with severe learning disabilities came to live at Queen Mary's. They came from the Fountain Hospital in Tooting, which was a fearful old Mental Handicap Hospital where hundreds of children had lived for years in sordid huts. Many had been kept in cots all the time, but others had gone to occupation huts every day, where they did tasks such as putting pegs into boards or threading beads.

As the Fountain Hospital was so awful it was thought a compassionate decision to close it and move the children to Queen Mary's. At that time people did not think about planning community care; most new ideas concentrated on how to improve institutional care – hence the move from the Fountain to Queen Mary's. Queen Mary's was better, of course, than the Fountain. It was in a more beautiful setting, with trees, lawns and flower beds, and the villas were brick-built. But it was still an institution, and the staff who came from the Fountain brought with them the old institutional patterns of care. So, in effect, the children had moved from one institution to another.

Some of the girls with learning disabilities who had grown up in the Fountain had gone in their late teens to live in a Home called Southside in Streatham, and they were driven to Queen Mary's in a coach every day to help look after the children with learning disabilities. These women from Southside were all dressed in pink dresses, pinnies, white ankle socks and flat sandals; and they had very short hair-cuts. They were known as the 'Pink Ladies'.

They used to go to the villas and do cleaning or help to spoon feed children who could not feed themselves. They were being exploited to work in the hospital looking after the children, for just a pittance of pocket money. Maybe some of these 'Pink Ladies' did not even like working with children, maybe they would have preferred to work in a shop or a café, but I'm sure they were not asked. They had grown up in institutional care and they remained to work in institutions.

Gradually, I began to get the occasional child with severe learning disabilities in my little group of children with cerebral palsy. The current Education Act did not include 'severely subnormal children' in ordinary education, so by accepting children with severe learning disabilities into my group I was stretching the Education laws; I was a Ministry of Education qualified teacher working in a local education authority financed hospital school, but the more severely disabled children who had come from the Fountain were categorised as 'ineducable' and only eligible for having occupation under the supervision of unqualified teachers.

The head teacher once appeared in my room and looked in horror at a child with severe learning disabilities in my group. 'But this child is severely subnormal,' she cried out. The legal education wheels then turned and the child was transferred to the Foundation section of the hospital. Officials liked to sort out such muddles of administration and they soon weeded out any child who had slipped from the pigeon hole into which society had placed him.

Gradually, I began to criticise the care of the children in my particular villa. I asked if I could take them to town. 'But *these sort* of children do not *GO OUT,*' the head teacher said. And the older teachers warned me, 'Do not get yourself emotionally involved with the children.'

As my criticisms of the hospital grew stronger I grew unpopular. My colleagues complained that I was being 'disloyal'. I was in particular trouble for writing to the Hospital Management Committee and to Enoch Powell (then Minister of Health) to say that I needed a better room in which to teach my children.

The head teacher eventually said that I was 'mad' and would be black-listed on my teacher's records and never receive promotion. (I never did, and in the end this affected my Retirement Pension.)

As time went on I got all sorts of little improvements for the children, such as regular outings to town, bits of furniture for the bedroom, and even a tiny cooker in my school-room so they could enjoy mixing up flour to make cakes.

In the late 1960s I met Jack Tizard, well-known for his research into the effects of institutional care on child development. I talked to him about the children at Queen Mary's and he obtained a small grant of about £150 for me to do some part-time research. The grant came from the Spastics Society (now SCOPE) and helped to pay my expenses in travelling to look at other institutions caring for children with disabilities.

As I was still working at Queen Mary's and could not take time off, I had to do the study at weekends. Jack said that would be no bad thing because he was sure that weekends were a special time of deprivation for children in institutions.

So every Friday afternoon I would leave Queen Mary's about five o' clock and visit another Hospital, Home or Boarding School and work there for the weekend. On Monday mornings I would be at Queen Mary's again. It meant that for a few months I was working a seven-day week but it did not seem tiring as I was very committed.

My book about those weekend studies was called *'The Empty Hours'*.[241] It was published in August 1971 and received masses of publicity. I had not expected that local papers all over the country, as well as the big national dailies, would run stories about my book and produce headlines such as, 'Exposure of neglect in children's hospital'. I had to do interviews on radio and TV and kept on saying how there were children living deprived lives all over the country. At the time there were some 12,000 children living in long-stay hospitals.

I had such a lot of publicity that I felt shy about returning to Queen Mary's after the summer holidays. I thought that my colleagues would want to know all about my work. Instead, I found that many of them were angry about the book, they muttered things about 'loyalty to one's workplace and colleagues' and were not a bit concerned about the children I had described. They never said, 'Oh, Maureen's told us about these children, how awful, we must do something.' They merely grumbled, 'she should not have written these things.'

One of the worst sights I had seen when I was doing my weekend research concerned a small group of children who had no arms or legs because they had been damaged by the drug thalidomide before birth. The children lived in a very institutionalised hospital and every morning at 4.00 a.m. they were lifted from their cots and placed on little potties to have a pee. They were sometimes left on these pots, all in a row on concrete floors, for over an hour. And they cried bitterly in distress because they could see cockroaches crawling on the floor beside them.

There were these armless and legless little children aged five, balanced on little pots on dark winter mornings on concrete floors infested with cockroaches; and there were my colleagues saying, 'you have been disloyal.' Where did my loyalties lie? With the neglected children or with colleagues who had their heads in the sand?

I left Queen Mary's in 1974 and spent the next few years working at the Thomas Coram Research Unit, where Jack Tizard was Director. My first research project was visiting big long-stay Mental Handicap hospitals to observe the care of the children who lived in what were called Special Care Wards. All Mental Handicap hospitals had Special Care Wards, which usually housed twenty or thirty children who had severe physical disabilities in addition to learning disabilities. The majority of the children could not speak, could not hold anything in their hands, could not walk or feed themselves, some of them were blind and many were physically deformed.

If the staff had walked out of the Special Care Wards and had not gone back for a couple of days, the children would still have been in the same places in the day-room – lying on mattresses and bean bags, or slumped half out of their wheelchairs, none would have been able to seek help, food, water or warmth. They were that helpless.

It is very important that we remember these children who lived in the Special Care Wards. When we talk about exclusion we have to understand that in all institutions there will be groups within groups, and the most deprived and excluded group of people in the old Mental Handicap hospitals were those who had multiple disabilities. Their wards were rarely seen.

Today, when most of the long-stay hospitals have been shut and people are living in the community and are telling their stories, there are those who can describe their earlier lives and say, 'I spent years living in an institution, I was very deprived.' They can put up their hands and say, 'Remember my story.' But the children I worked with will never be able to put up their hands and tell their stories. When the final history of the old Mental Handicap hospitals is written not one of those people with multiple disabilities who grew up in Special Care Wards will be able to stand up and say what it was like to be so deprived for so long, to be so excluded, so forgotten by society.

When I was doing the Special Care Ward research I would stay in a hospital for four to six weeks and live in staff accommodation. I would work on the children's ward all day from about 6.00 a.m., helping to wash and dress the children, giving them cuddles, trying to play with them, helping them to eat their food and have their drinks, and observing their care.

As I spent such a lot of time on the wards I got to know the children and their care systems very well, and when I got back to my room at about ten at night I used to write up my notes of the children's daily life. Thinking about it now I wonder where I found the energy to work such long hours, but when you are committed to doing something and you know that there is neglect which needs exposing, you do work up a lot of energy.

The Special Care Ward children were aged from about three to eighteen, but they were often called 'babies' by the hospital staff and the other residents. Now I am raking up labels which people who have not worked in institutions may not know anything about: such as 'high-grades' and 'low-grades' and 'babies'. 'High-grades' were people who could walk about and could do a job such as gardening, cleaning, or working in stores or kitchens. But Special Care Ward children were always known as 'babies' or 'low-grades' or even as 'cot-and-chair-cases'. This last description was often said very quickly, to sound like 'cotten-chorcase'. The first time I heard this I asked, 'What is "cotton-chorcase"?' It simply meant 'a cot-and-chair-case', a human being of any age, who was never got out of his cot or his chair. Some of the older staff remembered the days when children with multiple handicaps were called 'basket cases' because they were kept in baskets.

Most of the children labelled 'babies' or 'low-grades' spent all day lying on mattresses or bean bags, or they sat slumped in wheel-chairs. Their physical positions were appalling, some were screwed into foetal positions for so many years that their spines became permanently curled and their legs could not be straightened. It was very depressing to see these young people with such terrible deformities which could have been prevented by early physiotherapy advice.

The children would be vaguely grouped round the television, which ran from one boring programme to another all day, bizarrely flickering through umpteen soap operas and world crises, not understood or even watched by the children.

Sometimes a child in the group became the staff 'pet', because he could shove his wheelchair along or had been taught to say some cheeky catch-phrase. He would then be allowed into the ward office, where the Charge Nurse would be reading the tabloids and having a smoke. The favoured child would sit there and maybe have a sip of coffee or even beer. Some of the 'pet' children were even given puffs of cigarettes, which made the staff laugh.

As well as being dreadfully deformed through lack of physiotherapy, some of the children developed poor skins due to lack of fresh air and nutritious fresh fruit and vegetables. The majority of the children also suffered a degree of dehydration because they could not get access to drinks and the staff did not spend the time which was necessary to help them to drink. Nobody seemed to realise that they were nearly always thirsty and that a few quick sips of tea or orange juice from baby-beakers at breakfast, lunch and supper were insufficient. I have seen teenage boys, who were able to drag themselves about on their knees, go into ward courtyards and suck at puddles.

The children's lack of loving one-to-one care was one of the saddest aspects of their lives. I logged up how much personal attention they received daily, such as talking to, cuddling and playing with, and found that for most of the children it was as little as five minutes in twelve hours. And that attention was often from the cleaning staff who would be sweeping the floor and they would pat a child on the shoulder and say, 'you're a good boy, aren't you,' or from the men bringing food dishes from the Central Kitchen who might bang on the windows and shout greetings. That would be the only individual attention received by many of the children for year after year – just passing taps on the shoulder and passing shouts through windows. They were totally excluded from all normal childhood experiences.

The book which I wrote about life in Special Care Wards was called *Children Living in Long-stay Hospitals* and was published in 1978. The cover design showed a drawing of a typical ward scene, taken from the notebooks I kept.

The book had a lot of publicity and there was an unexpected uproar from the Nursing Union called COHSE. Some members of this Union were hard-line bolshie male nurses and they would turn up in force at conferences where I was speaking. They sometimes joined with staff from the Special Hospitals and would hassle in a most aggressive manner. They were not interested in the deprived lives of the children. They just saw my criticism as a threat to their own careers, being afraid that campaigns to close hospitals might eventually succeed.

I remember a Conference in Exeter, organised by MENCAP, where a particularly nasty group of male nurses crowded into the hall, determined to disrupt the meeting. Peggy Jay was chairing it and she too came in for barracking because of her work in recommending changes in nurse training. Afterwards, sitting at Exeter Station, Peggy and I laughed at the masterly way in which she had kept control of the difficult audience.

Not only nurses, but doctors were disagreeable about any criticism of the long-stay hospitals. They said that the children in Special Care Wards needed to live in hospitals because they 'required constant medical and nursing care'. My answer was to point out that the children never actually received any 'medical and nursing care' and that their general health was suffering because of their neglect.

It amazed me how nurses and doctors constantly denied that the children were neglected both physically and emotionally. Now, when I see TV pictures about Eastern European hospitals, I think, 'yes, that is how it was for our children in our hospitals only twenty years ago.' Our children were not two in a bed, but there was the same steady neglect: children crying, rocking, crawling about dirty and dribbling, nobody sitting them up properly and talking to them or wiping their mouths and noses, nobody giving them a drink and a cuddle.

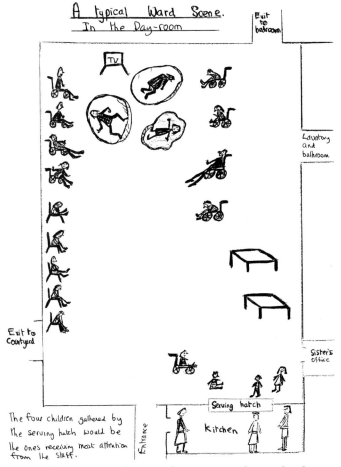

Figure 15 - Extract from research notebook

At a personal level, talking about exclusion, any sense of exclusion I sometimes felt at the time, it is now so much water under the bridge. I spoke out, so I suppose I was an early form of 'whistle-blower' but such a label had not then been invented. What happened to me, however, was peanuts compared to the exclusion which those Special Care Ward children suffered for their entire childhood.

I will finish with reference to a child I met in a Lancashire hospital in the 1970s. He was then about twelve years old and he would crawl about and catch hold of the knees of staff and pull himself up and stare silently into our faces. He could not speak. All he could do was to pull himself up and stare. For today, I will call him Thomas.

About thirteen years after working in that hospital I went back to give a seminar. I was told that changes had been made, people had moved out and wards were shut. The staff suggested that I visited the Special Care Ward where I had worked on my research. When I got there I could see that there had been changes: pretty counter-panes, partitioning to make privacy, and there were no longer any small children living there. Then I saw Thomas. He was still there, still crawling about the floor, still catching hold of people's knees – but now he was in his mid-twenties, with a dark beard and his hair starting to recede. He grabbed my knees and stared into my face. I just did not know what to say. He could not speak. I was powerless to help him. What could either of us do?

Thomas was one of the many people who have remained excluded. When we congratulate ourselves on achievements in community care, remember this group of people who cannot speak or walk, who once lived in children's Special Care Wards. They were excluded for all their childhood and many of them remain excluded in adulthood.

---

[241] Maureen Oswin, *The Empty Hours,* (London. Allen Lane: The Penguin Press, 1971).

[242] Maureen Oswin, *Children Living in Long-Stay Hospitals,* (London: Heinemann Medical, 1978) Spastics International Medical Publications Research Monograph No. 5.

[243] Great Britain, Parliament, *Report of the Committee of Enquiry into Mental Handicap Nursing and Care* (Chairman Peggy Jay), (London: HMSO, 1979), Cmnd, 7468-1.

Chapter 11

Leaving a convent home: different communities, different voices

Mary Stuart

In this chapter, Mary Stuart examines the views of four women, labelled as having learning difficulties, who crossed the boundary from a long-stay residential convent home to live in the wider community. She argues that the women's attitudes to community living differed, depending upon their personal feelings about convent life and their experiences of the wider community. Boundaries can take many forms, including physical or geographical, cultural and personal. The stories told by the women in this chapter refer in some way to all of these boundaries and the author suggests that the changes related to boundary crossings are always connected to people's personal, social or cultural identities. Therefore, decisions made about choice of lifestyle for people with learning difficulties should not only focus on practical issues, such as where to live and budgeting skills, but should explore how moving between different physical environments affects people's sense of who they are. Finally, the chapter argues that personal relationships and networks seem to be more important in finding a sense of place than physical environment itself.

Hearing different voices – a life-history approach

The accounts described in this research are based on life-history interviews with women who lived in a convent for most of the twentieth century. Many of the residents were placed in the convent by family members who were unable or unwilling to care for them. Most residents came to live in the convent as teenagers and so, for most of the women, convent life dominated their experience.

Life-history research poses many challenges. Its main objective is to give voice to people's experiences but this is not a simple matter and, like all research, it is shot through with questions of power. Chouinard and Grant point out that, in working with disempowered people, questions of power and the privileging of knowledge need to be examined. As researchers we need to ensure that we 'hear' what we are being told and that the narrative we present in research is true to the stories we are told. Chouinard and Grant[244] go on to argue that research design should include informants' 'interpretations' as '... the researcher and participants live the research process in a very direct way.'[245] This sort of research design acknowledges different understandings and places weight on the expert knowledge of those who have lived the experience. While this research method does not solve all the difficulties of unequal power relations in research it does provide a more participatory approach.

Many stories of the closures of long-stay hospitals indicate that if people with learning difficulties were 'given three wishes' they would be 'to be out'[246] and biographies from people with learning difficulties have emphasised the prisonlike quality of such institutions.[247] The principle of 'normalisation' and consequent emphasis on 'ordinary houses in ordinary streets,'[248] suggests that moving out of long-stay institutions was unproblematic. However, in life-history research, where the expert is the person who has lived the experience, a number of different narratives can emerge. As well as the perception of institutions being like prisons, there are also accounts which highlight contradictory attitudes to closure – in particular, where people feel that their identity has become shaped by the institution and its practices.[249] Opie[250] noted that, within some life-history texts, there are contradictory stories being told. It is our complexity that makes us what we are and allowing for differences within individuals creates a rich and textured research story. This means that, in any boundary crossing, people may have ambivalent feelings about the change. In research, it is therefore important to ensure that we not only 'hear' one version of a person's story, but also allow for contradictions and nuances.

The following accounts highlight the different perspectives of women who shared a similar living environment but whose relationships to this environment differed. It highlights, from their own accounts of their changing lives, how their identities were shaped by these relationships and how their prior cultural and social affiliations affected their engagement with the wider community. To gain a picture of people's experiences and perceptions of their lives takes time and requires trust. This is especially the case when people's sense of themselves is being challenged, as it is in any boundary crossing. This research was conducted over eight years, which gave me time to develop relationships, to re-interview the women as their lives changed and to include their interpretations of events. It also enabled me to observe the convent community through a period of major change, as legislation and the ethos of care for people with learning difficulties shifted to community living. When I began the research there were 80 women who lived in the convent and by the time I completed the research it had closed. Over the eight years I worked with 30 women to gather their histories and, through them, I built up a picture of the history of convent life from the early twentieth century till its closure.

Whose community and which identity?

Even in the 1980s and 1990s, convent life, as other forms of institutional life, was highly structured. Routines and daily rhythms dominated the women's lives. Many of these daily routines were centred on Catholic ritual, feast days, Mass, the Catholic calendar and retreats. This pattern of existence created the cultural and personal boundaries of the women who lived in the convent. While there were unique practices in the convent that made daily life different to people's lives outside, since the 1960s the women had increasingly been able to participate in more general social activities. Television was a popular pastime and visits to the shops and adult education centres brought the women into contact with modern British life. Lay staff, who were not religious, were employed as carers within the convent, which also altered relationships between the

149

residents and the Sisters. Despite these changes, the specifics of convent life meant that the women's experiences continued to be different to those of other people. Policy changes made the move from segregated care to inclusive living an imperative and closure of the convent therefore became inevitable.

As the residents were moved out of the convent I discussed with them their attitudes to living in the wider community. Each person had their own feelings and attitudes; most were a mix of emotions but three main positions emerged from my interviews. One theme that emerged was a positive response to moving out of the convent. The women who responded in this way felt that the convent was a prison and that they had been contained and limited by both its physical and religious boundaries. Another group felt quite differently. They wished to remain within the convent and saw the prospect of closure as a threat to their way of life. These women saw the regime and bounded nature of convent life as a sort of freedom, a way of knowing your 'place'. There was also a third group that wanted to move out of the convent buildings but also to maintain the support of the staff and the contacts and friendships they had developed over the years. This group of women was arguing for physical freedom, crossing from the containment of the convent to the outside world, but remaining within the social boundaries of their established networks. Each of these attitudes is represented in the life-stories of the four women in this chapter. The first story is of a young black woman, whom I call Jessica,[251] who wanted to leave the convent where she lived and who was able to successfully re-negotiate her life in the wider community.

Jessica, who was born in Jamaica, had been left at the convent by her parents as a teenager. She lost contact with her parents after she arrived at the convent and no longer knew where they were. She would often complain to me of the racism of the other women in the convent. She told me that her social worker had suggested she spoke to the Sisters but that she should 'remember that the other women don't understand when they call you Blackie.'[252] Jessica had lived in the convent until 1990 when she was encouraged to move out. She was confident in her use of money and studied word-processing at a local Further Education College. When the move was planned I asked her how she felt. She said:

I'm really pleased to be going. There is racism here. Some of the girls call you names. I'm getting on now and I'll be held back if I stay. I'm looking forward to making new friends.[253]

Jessica moved out and stayed in a boarding house. She was keen to break her ties with the convent and told me when I interviewed her six months after her move:

... I don't want to see the others. My life is different now. I like college and hang round with them.[254]

She went on to tell me she had become involved with the black students' group at the college and was finding out about her past. Jessica's ability to find another community identity seemed to be an important factor in her 'success' in living in the community. Jessica was able to do this by becoming involved in the black students' group. She was able to develop new friendships by claiming affiliation to another community who recognised her and offered her personal esteem and adult status. Jessica had achieved several successful boundary crossings: a personal one where she had developed a new sense of who she was as a black woman, a social one where she had found new affiliations to support her new sense of self, as well as physically shifting from one environment into another.

This is not always the case for people with learning difficulties. Ramcharan et al. point out that for most people with learning difficulties, 'full inclusion in society ... [will only be possible] when educational, community and work places are re-structured to enable that to happen.'[255] However, as indicated in the case study above, cultural and community affinities are also potentially significant factors in 'inclusion'. A successful transition for Jessica, between two worlds, required her to see herself differently and to have that sense of self affirmed by another community. For some of the women in the convent this was not possible. The following story highlights the loneliness that some people moving into the community experienced.

Susan was a young woman in her early twenties. She lived in the convent for six years, having been placed there in 1983 when she was 18, on the recommendation of a social worker. Her family could no longer accommodate her. After moving to the convent she maintained a troubled relationship with her mother but felt unwanted. She was always keen to leave the convent and told me,

'I don't believe in all this God stuff. Mass is a real drag. I can't wait to get out. I want a boyfriend like my sister.'[256] She was an able woman who was very articulate and she held down a part-time job as a cleaner. She moved into a hostel in London for young people with learning difficulties in the autumn of 1990. She made friends with one of the men in the hostel and became pregnant two months later. Susan was distressed. She said to me, 'I wanted a boyfriend, now I'm having a baby and he's gone and left me. I know what the Sisters think. They think it serves me right.'[257] Susan moved to a group home. Her baby was adopted. She continued to shift between part-time jobs and different relationships but told me when we met the next year, 'I've learnt now. I'm on the pill so it's okay.'[258] At this final interview she reflected on her life since leaving the convent:

> *When I was there I wanted to leave. I still wouldn't want to live there but there were some good bits. It's a bit frightening living like I do now. They've cut my benefit so I have to work now, but sometimes I don't feel like it and I like the boys but I've learnt they don't always treat you right. Sister always used to say that ... But I'm not unhappy, just a little lonely ... I don't have many friends.*[259]

Susan is not unlike many young working-class women working in part-time insecure jobs who are afraid of greater poverty. She was involved with a number of men but did not feel able to establish a permanent relationship with any of them. She was very lonely and, because she had lived in the convent in her late teens and early twenties, had never developed the friendship networks which sustain many women. She had no community ties to draw on and, therefore, despite living in the community, she was unable to find her place within the community. She had been able to shift from the boundaries of the convent but was now bound by the limiting factors of poverty and loneliness. Susan was living in a state of 'in-betweenness'.[260] She was physically located within 'the wider community' but not a part of any community.

The following two stories are from older women in the convent who were devout Catholics. Their responses to living in the wider community differed according to their perceptions of Catholicism and this further highlights the importance of cultural and community affinity.

Amanda was born in London in 1890 and came to live in the convent after she had had an illegitimate child at the age of fourteen. In 1954 she moved from the convent to a long-stay mental handicap hospital, where she lived until 1988, and then she moved into a group home. The hospital, like the convent, had been segregated and several convent Sisters had stayed in contact with Amanda when she lived in the hospital and, later, when she moved into the group home. I met her in 1989, when she attended a reminiscence group that I facilitated at the convent. When I asked her how she liked her new home, she became tearful and told me, 'I want to come and live here. I want to live with the Sisters'.[261] She found the group home difficult and did not enjoy living with men for the first time in her life, 'They smell and are dirty. They say filthy things.'[262] She missed going to mass; 'no-one will take me,' she said. I spoke with her care worker who told me that Amanda's difficulty was that she had been used to going to mass regularly in her previous home. Her current staff did not have the resources to get her to a service so frequently. When Amanda was asked where she would like to go for her holidays she asked if she could stay at the convent, 'then I can go to mass every day.'[263]

Thirty years on, with experience of a number of different lifestyles, she still wanted to live in a convent. The traditional preparation for 'independent living' – cookery, money management, and so on – did not offer Amanda the preparation she needed to move from a female environment, that was structured within strict boundaries with ritual and religious symbols, to an environment which was centred on a secular modern world. If independent living is to be successful, the symbolic meanings which individuals have lived through, and by, need to be understood and valued. For Amanda, her sense of herself as a devout Catholic was of great importance. She saw the convent as a space where she could express herself. For her, the convent was the community that she wished to embrace. Shifting from a woman-only environment to a mixed-sex environment was equally difficult for her. Hence, for Amanda, her dislike of changing boundaries was not only related to her religious and cultural affiliations but also to her prior experience of living with women. Her boundary change occurred at a time when mixed-sex environments in group homes were encouraged.[264] The principle of 'normalisation' which placed emphasis on 'ordinary houses in ordinary streets'[265] also privileged heterosexual lifestyles.

The final story of community living comes from Martha who was a devout Catholic but never thought her Catholicism should mean 'a life apart'. Martha came to the convent in 1947. Having spent several years in Ghana, where her father was a school teacher, she returned to England because of illness. She then spent a life in institutions: convent boarding school till 1945, and then later a farm school. On one occasion, when I was interviewing Martha, I asked her if she would elaborate on the reasons for entering the convent:

MS:　　When we talked before, Martha, you said your parents had told you should come here [the convent] because you cried a lot, was that the only reason?

Martha:　Well I had lots of tests at school, I had to see the psychologist twice and he said my I.Q. wasn't up to scratch and you see when I was four my mother had a nervous breakdown and the social worker found us and we were both just screaming and the social workers said I should go to boarding school. Boarding school from four, then Tattingstone, then on here.[266]

When I first met Martha, in 1992, she was already being 'trained' to move out. In 1993, Martha moved from the main convent building to a flat owned by the movement down the road from the main convent site. She was very happy. Her Catholicism was tied to the parish community. She was an active member in the women's group in the parish and in 1993 she was elevated to being a 'Eucharist Minister'[267] in the church. Martha's attitude to living in the community was positive. As she said, 'I really do like being independent.'[268] The independence which Martha developed was supported by a number of different opportunities. In September 1994 she moved into a bedsit of her own in an unsupported home. She became assistant tutor on adult education courses in local history and computing and co-led a reminiscence group with me. As Martha said in the autobiography which she produced, 'I go up to the convent every day from Monday to Fridays to do my charges so you see I am not lonely and it suits me fine.'[269] She had a range of support networks and shifted between friends and contacts in the parish community and the convent.

In December 1994, Martha became ill. She told me, 'I don't know what it is, the doctor says I've been eating too much ...'[270] Martha was taken to hospital in the middle of January 1995. She was diagnosed with cancer, with a maximum of a year to live. When I visited her later that month, she was saying her rosary, a set of Catholic prayers. She told me as we discussed her condition, 'That'll teach me to do so much, to expect so much.' I argued that she should not see the disease as punishment. She continued:

> *I wonder if I should have said the things I've told you and there's the autobiography. I don't know .... I wonder if this is God's punishment. I mean I feel ashamed of what I've said. The Sisters are good people. I've been thinking about the mass I went to for the Order last year. I remember all the things the priests said about the Sisters, all the wonderful work they have done with the poor and people who have got problems and I feel ashamed. I wouldn't be good enough to be a nun. I believe I'm going to God you know. It's a comfort. I'm glad I have that to believe in.*[271]

Martha did change some of the stories in her autobiography. She said in the final version:

> *I came to realise what wonderful people the Sisters had always been to everyone who were poor and had problems and I began to feel ashamed of my self.*[272]

Martha died in March 1995. Her funeral was held in the local Catholic Church. Despite holding over two hundred seats, the priest had to squeeze in extra chairs. Martha had clearly made an impression on her local Catholic community. At the service people spoke of Martha's dedication to the parish and her work for the convent. It was an emotional service and she was later buried in the grounds of the convent.

In her last few weeks, Martha had felt guilt about her challenges to the convent. She had needed to come to terms with her life and illness and this was one way she felt she needed to express her complex emotions. Talking with her in her last few weeks made me more aware of the complex psychological experiences which the convent life had given many of the women. The convent had been more than an institution that provided a form of care that has now become outmoded. It had also provided a lifestyle that affected the residents' identities and ways of seeing the world. Therefore, moving out of the convent was not just about crossing physical boundaries but also about shifting cultural, social and personal boundaries that dramatically affected the women's sense of who they were.

Dissolving boundaries – difference and different life styles

Some of the women in the convent had made sense of themselves through the symbolic language and culture of the convent. The women like Martha and Susan, who wanted to leave the convent, for quite different reasons, found that the symbols of Catholic convent life shaped the way they saw themselves. In other words, these women had developed identities over time that included the meanings inscribed in the Catholic culture of the convent.

The guilt that these women say they felt had negative effects. While Susan's behaviour was not uncommon amongst young women, she understood her behaviour through the eyes of the Sisters. Equally, Martha, at the end of her life, measured her pleasure in living in the wider community against her inability to appreciate the 'goodness' of the Sisters. This perhaps has implications for other 'spiritual communities', indicating a need to examine moral values and their impact on community members. It also has implications for other service provision, where taken-for-granted service practices also shape the identities and available options for residents.[273] Yet, on the other hand, Martha also found dignity through her religious beliefs. Her conviction that there was a life after death gave her strength through a difficult and destructive illness.

The meanings inscribed in the culture of the convent, and the deeply held religious beliefs that many of the women felt, also affected how these women were prepared for living in the wider community. As they moved out of the convent environment, these women needed to learn more than independent living skills, they needed some sense of the different culture in which they would be living. As Amanda's account illustrates, their supporters needed to understand the Catholic language the women had used to negotiate their lives. Cultural affinity and community links, where they existed, could provide positive support for community living, as shown by Jessica's story, and should be valued.

We are more aware in the 1990s of the need for a valuing of difference, but often do not see the complexity of experience within difference:

how difference shapes identity and can potentially limit our ability to appreciate options. The stories of these women, who had lived in the convent, highlight a diversity of values and show how our life-histories and experiences can shape our future and sense of our-selves. These issues need to be addressed if people with learning difficulties are to be able to live fulfilled lives in the future.

This chapter has argued that the traditional boundary of institution/community is not always useful and needs to be re-assessed. In the personal accounts, the convent could be either 'institution' or 'community' and the wider community could be more alienating in its lack of 'community'. For some, the strict boundaries of religious life can be supportive, and even give people a sense of who they are, while for others they can limit their potential. Crossing boundaries from one environment to another often requires a personal engagement with cultural practices and social behaviours which affects how successful these transitions can be for people. Acknowledging the diversity of experiences and the complexity of different community identities therefore challenges simplistic solutions for inclusion in 'the com-munity' and indicates that there is no one answer for social policies. Rather, there is a need to listen more closely to the diversity of experiences of people with learning difficulties in order to plan more person-centred life choices.

[244] V. Chouinard and A. Grant, 'Ways of Putting Ourselves in the Picture', in Duncan, N. (ed.), *Body Space: Destabilising Geographies of Gender and Sexuality,* (London: Routledge, 1996).

[245] Ibid., p.182

[246] M. Potts and R .Fido *A Fit Person to Be Removed: Personal Accounts of Life in a Mental Deficiency Institution,* (Plymouth: Northcote Press, 1991), p.119.

[247] M. Cooper, 'Mabel's Life Story', in D. Atkinson, M. Jackson and J. Walmsley (eds), *Forgotten Lives: Exploring the History of Learning Disability,* (Plymouth: BILD Publications, 1997).

[248] King's Fund, Ties and Connections: *An Ordinary Community Life for People with Learning Difficulties,* (London: Kings Fund Centre, 1988).

[249] D. Atkinson and F. Williams, *Know me as I am Am: An Anthology of Prose, Poetry and Art by People with Learning Difficulties,* (Sevenoaks: Hodder and Stoughton, 1990).

250 A Opie, 'Qualitative Research: Appropriation of the "Other" and Empowerment', in *Feminist Review,* 40, (Spring, 1992), 52-70.

251 All the names in this chapter are pseudonyms chosen by the women themselves to protect their identity.

252 Interview with Jessica conducted at the convent, 1990.

253 Ibid.

254 Interview with Jessica in her new home, 1991.

255 P. Ramcharan, G. Roberts, G. Grant and J. Borland, 'Citizenship, Empowerment and Everyday Life: Ideal and Illusion in the New Millennium', in P. Ramcharan, G. Roberts, G. Grant and J. Borland (eds), *Empowerment in Everyday Life: Learning Disability,* (London: Jessica Kingsley, 1997), p.256.

256 Interview with Susan at the convent, 1990.

257 Interview with Susan at the hostel, 1991.

258 Interview with Susan at group home, 1992.

259 Ibid.

260 H. Bhabha, *The Location of Culture,* (London: Routledge, 1994).

261 Interview with Amanda at the convent, 1990.

262 Ibid.

263 Ibid.

264 As noted in H. Brown and H. Smith (eds), *Normalisation: A Reader for the Nineties,* (London: Routledge, 1992).

265 King's Fund, 1988 (see note 248).

266 Interview with Martha at the convent, 1993.

267 Martha wrote her autobiography which was published under her real name, M. Adams, *Those Lost Years,* (Brighton: Queen Spark Market Books, 1995), p.48.

268 Interview with Martha while living independently, 1994.

269 M. Adams, *Those Lost Years,* p.48 (see note 267).

270 Interview with Martha at her home, 1995.

271 Interview with Martha in hospital, 1995.

272 M Adams, *Those Lost Years,* p.49 (see note 267).

273 S. Dowson, 'Empowerment within Services: A Comfortable Delusion', in *Empowerment in Everyday Life Learning Disability,* Ramcharan, P., Roberts, G., Grant, G. and Borland, J. (eds), (London: Jessica Kingsley, 1997).

274 Brown and Smith, *Normalisation,* 1992 (see note 264).

Chapter 12

Collecting the life-stories of self-advocates: crossing the boundary between researcher and researched

Dan Goodley,
in collaboration with
Jackie Downer, Patrick Burke, Joyce Kershaw, Lloyd Page and
Anya Souza

Summary

In this chapter Dan Goodley looks back on a research project that had two aims: (i) to give a voice to the insiders of the self-advocacy movement – people with learning difficulties or 'self-advocates', and (ii) to use the life story research method in a collaborative way with self-advocates. The life stories of Jackie Downer, Patrick Burke, Joyce Kershaw, Lloyd Page and Anya Souza were collected. These people were chosen to provide personal histories of self-advocacy because of their long-term involvement with self-advocacy groups. Writing their stories raised many issues for Dan, some of which are addressed in this chapter. The first section introduces the life-story and presents some of its advantages and disadvantages. The second section looks at ideas about interviewing and the reality of carrying out interviews. The third section considers how the stories of a few people with learning difficulties can be useful to many other people with learning difficulties. The final section looks at analysis and considers whether it is right to analyse the stories of others. In writing this chapter, Dan attempts to bridge the boundary between academic writing and accessible writing, to make sure that the ideas in it are open to all readers.

(1) Introduction: why are stories important?

For a number of years, researchers in psychology, sociology and social work have recognised that stories allow us a way of understanding people and the society that we live in. For example, Bowker says that we live in a time where stories are all around us.[277] Some researchers use the term 'narrative inquiry' to refer to the collection and use of stories in research.[278]

Narrative inquiry takes stories as the starting point for understanding such things as 'individuals', the 'family', the 'community', 'disability', 'self-advocacy', 'society' and 'personal and social history'. Some would say that a feature of human beings is that we are storytellers and that our lives can be seen as the acting out of many stories. Also we use stories to reflect on our lives – our histories. If we want to find out more about a person we should ask, then listen to the stories that they tell us. A result of this interest in 'narrative inquiry', is that over the last 30 years many stories have been collected by researchers. Some of these stories are the stories of people with learning difficulties. These include autobiographies, biographies, life-stories, oral histories and life-histories.[279] This chapter looks at the life-story.[280]

The life-story
A person's life-story includes a number of their life experiences put together in a storied, sometimes chronological, fashion. Life-stories can be written alone or told to researchers who help in the writing of the story. There are advantages and disadvantages in using life stories.

The advantages include:
Introducing the voice and histories of people with learning difficulties
When Whittemore, Langness and Koegel read through stories about people with learning difficulties, they found many stories by parents, carers and professionals but hardly any by people with learning difficulties.[281] A common assumption in our society is that people with learning difficulties are unable to talk about their lives. By presenting the life-stories of people with learning difficulties we ensure that their ideas, opinions and histories are no longer absent.

Checking out theories

Stories allow a personal sight of society.[282] A result of this is that the theories provided by researchers, psychologists, social workers and so on can be checked against stories. So, for example, previous understandings of self-advocacy put forward by professionals, supporters and researchers can be compared with the stories of self-advocates.

Story and meaning

Life-stories investigate some of the meanings held by storytellers, and also, by readers. Stories show some of the meanings that storytellers attach to their own experiences, while readers' own meanings are called upon in reflecting upon another's account. A knock-on effect may be that readers' own theories are looked at again in light of another's story. For example, stories of people with learning difficulties have falsified the assumption that the views of people with learning difficulties do not exist.[283] Bogdan and Taylor insist that life-stories enable us to understand society better, specifically to understand the meaning of disability.[284] On a more modest level, life-stories suited my aim of examining some of the meanings that people with learning difficulties had of 'self-advocacy' and self-advocacy groups.

Making the research process understandable

Research is a strange thing to explain to others.[285] One way of describing research is that it involves finding out things about society and individuals. Some researchers, like Tony Parker, say that when research involves telling stories, like life-story research, then it is easier to talk about research.[286] After all, we all know what storytelling is – we hear so many stories every day – and that is what life-story research is about.

The disadvantages of using life-stories include:

Only part of the story

Biographies are in a constant state of becoming. Today's story of a specific experience will read differently if told tomorrow. Life-stories are made up of a storyteller's reflections on some experiences from the past viewed at a time in the present. No single story can capture the range or richness of people's experiences.[287] Also, when life-stories are the product of collaborative relationships, as the aim was in my research, there is a danger that researchers only listen to certain stories and ignore other tales that are important to the storyteller.

Biased storytelling

Harrison and Stina-Lyon argue that the credibility of a person's story is the extent to which the story remains faithful to the reality of the storyteller.[288] However, all of us, as storytellers, make errors. We may exaggerate things, say we chose to do something when we were made to, rehearse stories or even lie. Some researchers say that we should check a person's story by asking their friends, family and other significant others.[289] However, it might not be right to ask if participants are telling the truth. Why people tell the stories that they tell may be more important, because behind the telling of stories are always intentions.[290]

Problems with relying on stories

Only being interested in some stories may ignore wider consider-ations.[291] For example, Whyte was criticised by Stott for totally accepting what his story-tellers ('the Cornerboys') told him. He remained, therefore, uncritical of their contempt, including the prejudiced views that they expressed.[292] Empathy with the stories of others can prove to be a weakness as well as a strength.

Problems with relying on story-tellers

Plummer argues that it is helpful to the narrative researcher if storytellers are able to speak clearly and for a long time about their lives. This preoccupation with articulate people has led to the exclusion of those that cannot tell or have difficulties telling stories. Even when 'inarticulate people' are included, researchers and others may take on dominant roles in the writing exercise. Questions remain about whose voice is dominant in the life-story.[293]

So, life-stories are not without their problems. Even so, I decided to use them and a rough plan of my research was drawn up and followed:

- Interview each person, or 'storyteller', to collect their stories.
- Ask each person about self-advocacy groups and how these groups have affected them in their lives.
- Tape-record the interviews, type up on a word processor what is recorded and write up what they say into a first draft of their life-story.
- Hand back the life-story for them to check.
- Edit the story together so as to end up with finished version that the storyteller is happy with.
- Add the life-story to my thesis.

(2) Interviewing and telling stories

I was fortunate enough to interview five storytellers who had extensive involvement with self-advocacy groups: Jackie Downer, Lloyd Page, Joyce Kershaw, Anya Souza and Patrick Burke. They taught me much about interviewing and about the need to cross boundaries: to move away from the notion that the interviewer has the expertise about collecting personal histories and instead to draw upon and follow the expertise of storytellers.

Contacting self-advocates

Storytellers were contacted by telephone and letter. During our first meetings I tried to explain my research with reference to an introductory booklet, which:
- Introduced the researcher.
- Explained how storytellers were helping me to write a thesis, i.e. a story of my research.
- Said what I would do with what they told me (I would write their life-stories in my thesis and, hopefully, in journals and books).
- Mentioned what both parties would get out of the research (their stories would help me write a thesis for my PhD, they would have their own stories to keep and, hopefully, I would publish their stories so that other people would know about self-advocacy).

Telling the storytellers about my involvement as a supporter to a self-advocacy group might have helped – as one storyteller put it, 'She didn't mind my sort'. We also discussed 'confidentiality' – things that they told me that they didn't want other people to know about would remain private. Finally, we talked about the need to 'preserve the anonymity of others' – changing the names of people that the storytellers mentioned who had not been asked by me if it was acceptable to include their names in the stories. All five story-tellers were proud to put their names to their life-stories.

About the interviews

All five storytellers were asked for their 'life-stories'. They told stories, either chronologically from childhood to adulthood, or thematically about certain topics (e.g. stories about day centres and then stories about family), but their stories were always interspersed with opinions.

Asking for stories, rather than experiences, may have encouraged more expression – perhaps it is easier to tell a story than to think of a number of events.[294] Interviews varied in length from about an hour and a half to five hours. Total contact time was longer. Interviews were carried out in a variety of places: at home, in restaurants, cafés and in a group office.[295]

Lofland says that the format and content of interviews should at all times be directed by the storyteller, while in contrast, Tremblay argues that interviewers have interests that they will want to explore in the interview.[296] I had some questions to ask, but they were used mainly as reminders and were not needed as central themes around which to organise chats. All storytellers spoke openly, gave short and long anecdotes, reflected on past experiences and considered present situations. However, storytellers did not just tell stories. Opinions and views were tangled up in their reflections on the past and present.

A problem – the over-enthusiastic interviewer

Taylor and Bogdan advise interviewers not to just sit there (saying nothing); not to direct the interview through enforcing their own opinions; to let people talk and listen to what they are saying; and to probe sensitively by asking questions in a thoughtful way.[297] Lloyd Page was the first person to be interviewed. Unfortunately, he was subjected to my over-enthusiastic questioning.

Lowe and de Paiva (1988) argue that storytellers with learning difficulties tend to reply with simple 'yes' or 'no' answers to questions. Atkinson (1989, 1993) found that frequently asking questions emphasised her interests and helped to build up trust and rapport with her storytellers. Also, O'Donnell, Flynn, and Flynn and Saleem all used direct questions to ascertain the views of people with learning difficulties.[298] I had read about research like this before I met Lloyd Page. Perhaps this literature was taken too literally into the interview with him. I was impatient, fired quick questions and gave him little time to respond. He said afterwards that he felt 'grilled like a tomato'. In contrast to Shakespeare, who felt that she had acted too naturally in her interviews,[299] Lloyd Page's interview highlighted problems with following the interviewing literature to the letter. Viewing Lloyd as a 'person with learning difficulties', who would respond best to a particular type of questioning, assumes that people with learning difficulties are all the same. Also, it seems to say that researchers have got it right about how to interview all people with learning difficulties. Indeed, Lawthom[300] has noted how researchers often go into their research with the idea that they know best. We should remember that good storytellers are rarely found, rather they emerge in the course of their everyday activities, not in artificially contrived research contexts.[301] Lloyd Page reminded me that I was seeing myself as an 'expert' and that I really needed to cross the boundary from expert to novice to learn from Lloyd's expertise.

The pros and cons of talking naturally
Thanks to Lloyd Page, the other storytellers were approached in a more 'natural' way. I tried to strike up conversations in the same way that I would with my friends and made use of leading questions as well as open questions. Some literature that deals with interviewing people with learning difficulties suggests that leading questions are inappropriate. The reasoning behind this claim is the reported tendency of people to answer 'yes' to questions regardless of their content.[302] To think that people with learning difficulties will always unquestionably say 'yes' assumes that they know no better. Perhaps, when people just say 'yes' it is because they feel powerless.[303] The storytellers in my research did not just say yes to leading questions – perhaps because of their involvement in self-advocacy and feeling in control of the interview process[304].

Joyce Kershaw ignored or spoke over some of my queries. Anya Souza presented long anecdotes that kept my questions to a minimum. Patrick Burke queried questions, 'Say that again,' and asked me to say a word that he couldn't, 'Vulnerable? That's right – that's the word.' Lloyd Page had obviously got sick of my grilling and stopped the interview by turning on the TV. We should remember that leading questions are a necessary part of the exchange of information between two people. In this sense, acting as 'naturally' as possible in interviews is a condition under which people come to know each other.[305] The better 'the chat' the more leading the questions. The trouble is, acting naturally has implications. Storytellers' words were often reactions to my leading questions and value-laden responses. These 'natural exchanges' were used in constructing narrative. Consequently, my words may have unnecessarily littered the interview material that was later used for writing stories. With hindsight I could have balanced my reactions to disclosures by keeping my opinions to myself.

The presence of other people
In a couple of the interviews other people were present in addition to the storyteller. Interviews can benefit from the presence of others but interviewees might not. Lloyd Page's mother offered her opinions and reminiscences. At times, they disagreed. I felt tense in the interview and anxious that she was talking over her son. When I listened to the tape recording of the interview, I felt less concerned. Her words only appeared now and then and when they did appear added to the large amount of material supplied by Lloyd.

In Patrick Burke's interview, one of his supporters was present throughout. The supporter sat in the office drawing up a poster and only spoke when Patrick threw a comment her way, such as 'Do you know we haven't got the beds in our house yet,' or when Patrick was down on himself and said, 'I'm getting there slowly,' and she replied, 'You're doing a great job'. Patrick used the supporter as a resource. I expect that Lloyd Page also appreciated his mother being present and I was the one with the worries. People with learning difficulties have strong voices and lots of things to say, which are not so easily stifled by other people.

Personal documents, taped and written notes
According to Tremblay, a good interview develops the storyteller's skills to recall facts and situations, stimulates memory and facilitates the expression of recollections. Familiar things and places enhance story-telling and reflections on personal biographies. Anya Souza showed me around her house, pointed to pictures of her family and her latest collection of stained glass works. Joyce Kershaw lent me a book in which she had co-written a chapter. We walked around her flat and she directed me to the war memorabilia that her brother had emblazoned across the walls. Coffee was made. The dining table was cleared. Lloyd Page brought down various leaflets from his bedroom. He showed me a pot racoon given to him and other delegates at the 1993 International People First conference. His mother cooked me a lovely meal and we all three of us had a chat after the interview. Jackie Downer and I sat at her usual table in the restaurant. She broke off from the interview to talk to the waitress. Patrick Burke skirted over the posters presented on the walls of his

office. He pointed out pictures of peers at conferences and coffee cups with odd designs.

Photographs, pictures, personal memorabilia and possessions can spark off discussion.[306] Familiarity can promote informality. By contrast, tape-recording may have emphasised the esoteric nature of research. One informant appeared to be uncomfortable when the tape-recorder was placed before them. I stopped it many times. Other storytellers did not seem so disconcerted. Written notes were taken with one storyteller because the tape-recorder was not working. Writing down what was said appeared to enforce some structure on conversations. The storyteller took the opportunity to re-phrase things she had said, to give more precise and thought-out reactions, and to indicate links with experiences that had been written down earlier. In addition, she stopped me a couple of times from writing down what she had said, asking me to re-phrase it or simply not include it in my notes. There are lots of ways to help the collection of stories. It would seem that being flexible is the best policy.

(3) How many stories: do researchers need to collect lots of stories to find out about self-advocacy?

All the storytellers I spoke to have been involved with self-advocacy groups for years. They are well known in the movement, some nationally, all locally. If self-advocacy has a history then it would be expected that the history of the movement would show up in storytellers' active engagement with the movement. This engagement came through in their narratives. However, their life-stories are not accounts of 'typical' self-advocates. The five storytellers are high profile, experienced, articulate members of the self-advocacy movement. Their stories are limited because they are not representative of the experiences of all self-advocates. So how useful are a few stories?

Humphreys, Evans and Todd collected seven life-stories of people with learning difficulties involved in the NIMROD services in Wales. About this small number of stories they argued:

> *While every description is very individual in nature, issues such as the struggle for basic rights as citizens can be seen in each account.*[308]

Similarly, the stories I collected were used to draw out conclusions that reflected, in a generalised form, what, in each document, was expressed in an individualised form.[309] Themes that emerged from one account were scrutinised against other accounts, allowing me in some small way to understand self-advocacy. Stories highlight some of the impacts of social history (in this case self-advocacy), on the life experiences of a few people, but are potentially of relevance to many.[310]

The argument that all stories can be dismissed, because they do not represent the experiences of all self-advocates with learning difficulties, is challenged by Michael Kennedy, a high profile and vocal American self-advocate. He offers the following response to those who say he is not talking for all people with learning difficulties:

> *When people tell me that I am 'higher functioning' than the people they are talking about, I feel like they are telling me that I don't have anything in common with other people with disabilities. It's like they are putting me in a whole different category and saying that I don't have any right to speak. It upsets me because I take it that they don't want to give anyone else the opportunities I have been given, and what I say they can ignore because I am more capable.*[311]

To say that only 'articulate people with learning difficulties' are able to get their stories written up ignores the collaborative nature of life-story research while also hinting at the idea that only certain people are able or 'articulate enough' to tell their stories. Five life stories are not representative of all self-advocates' experiences, but what is a 'typical account'? This question is impossible to answer when people with learning difficulties are all so very different.[310]

(4) Analysing stories: do researchers need to say anything about the stories?

Researchers in the fields of narrative inquiry and oral history are split over what to do with stories. Should they just present stories for readers and leave it at that? Or should they present stories for readers and then point out some of the things that those stories tell us about the history of people with learning difficulties and, in my case, self-advocacy? To point out some of the things that stories tell us about history, is to engage in 'analysis', and there are arguments for and against analysis.

Arguments for analysing stories[313]
The meanings of a story arise out of the interaction between the story, storyteller and audience.[314] What audiences do with stories is often unclear, so an argument may be made for analysis that points out to readers certain themes within stories. Goodson says that analysis should increase the wider benefits of stories by opposing unsympathetic, conservative or hostile readings.[315] The insider view of the storyteller and the analytical skills of the researcher are combined to draw out ideas.[316] For example, Levine and Langness concluded that the narratives of people with learning difficulties demonstrated a number of things; people so labelled are not all the same, that learning difficulties is a label created by society and that people have abilities which are often ignored.[317] Drawing out points of convergence in a number of stories shows the relevance of a few accounts to many similar others.[318] Stories cannot stand alone. Analysis strengthens stories and a history of learning difficulties.

Arguments against analysing stories[319]
If stories constitute 'the perfect sociological material',[320] then why analyse them? Analysis emphasises theory rather than stories, takes away ownership and privileges abstract interpretations and others' understandings of history; and perhaps rebuilds boundaries crossed in interviews. Simone Aspis, formerly Campaigns Officer for People First London, argues that when researchers draw conclusions from the stories of people with learning difficulties, then stories become secondary to researchers' 'expert' theories.[321] The subversive character of stories should not be underestimated. As people re-write their own stories this constitutes an important political step forward, as narratives extend each reader's sense of what it may mean to be human.[322] Allport says that social progress may come about through the employment of vivid stories of personal experience, just as came about through socially-orientated novels such as *Uncle Tom's Cabin, Oliver Twist* and *The Grapes of Wrath*.[323] Proponents in this camp conclude that analysis is an unnecessary preoccupation of researchers. As the self-advocacy movement has taught, stories display histories from which futures can be built.

Analysis as an aside and addition to stories[324]
So what to do then? Well, as far as I see it, the arguments presented by both camps can be accepted. In my research, the life-stories stood alone as separate chapters in my thesis and could be viewed without reference to the next chapter, which explored my reading of what I thought could be learnt from the stories about being in self-advocacy groups – that is, *my analysis.*[325] The nature of my commentary was twofold. Firstly, analysis was story-driven. Themes that emerged in stories were used to make sense of the lived historical experiences of self-advocacy, in turn highlighting points in the literature associated with self-advocacy and the social model of disability. Secondly, this literature was used to highlight anecdotes in the life-stories. I would argue that researchers should not feel that they are maintaining boundaries when they analyse without the involvement of story-tellers. Nevertheless, this should not mean that analysis remains researcher-driven, as recent examples of participatory narrative research have shown.[326] I would suggest that places exist for both *researcher-led* and *storyteller-led* research in the history of learning difficulties, so long as researchers clearly state which stance they are taking and don't pretend that they are involved in some form of research that they clearly are not. One thing to keep in mind, *whatever the stance,* is that people who have been given the label of 'learning difficulties' are still speaking up for themselves despite others' attempts to label and control them. Moreover, in attempting to write a history of learning difficulties, personal histories of people with learning difficulties provide the necessary start, middle and end points of this project. We should ensure that our own understandings of history parallel the lived realities of history.

Conclusion

My research and my attendance at the Social History of Learning Disability Conference, *Inclusion and Exclusion,* reminded me that people with learning difficulties are already speaking up for themselves and constructing their own histories: in self-advocacy groups, in service settings, with friends and family and with researchers. Jackie Downer, Patrick Burke, Joyce Kershaw, Lloyd Page and Anya Souza gave me insights into the first-hand experiences of self-advocacy. We should remember then, that a history of learning difficulties, of which self-advocacy is an integral part, can only be gained when researchers talk to these experts – people with learning difficulties – and so cross research boundaries.

[275] For more details please contact the author at Bolton Institute, Discourse Unit, Department of Psychology, Deane Campus, Bolton, BL3 5AB (Email: dag1@bolton.ac.uk) or see the following articles (all D. Goodley): 'Tales of Hidden Lives: A Critical Examination of Life History Research with People who have Learning Difficulties', Disability and Society, 11(3), (1996), 333-348; 'Supporting People with Learning Difficulties in Self-advocacy Groups and Models of Disability', *Health and Social Care in the Community*, 6(5), (1998), 438-446; *The Politics of Resilience: Self-advocacy in the Lives of People with Learning Difficulties*, (Buckingham: Open University Press, forthcoming).

[276] The term 'learning difficulties' is chosen in this chapter, as opposed to other related synonyms, such as mental handicap, mental impairment and learning disabilities. This reflects the preferred terminology of the self-advocacy movement in Britain. As one self-advocate clearly states, 'If you put people with "learning difficulties" then they know that people want to learn and to be taught how to do things', quoted in J. Sutcliffe and K. Simons, *Self-advocacy and Adults with Learning Difficulties: Contexts & Debates*, (Leicester: The National Institute of Adult Continuing Education in Association with The Open University Press, 1993).

[277] See G. Bowker, 'The Age of Biography is upon us', in *Times Higher Education Supplement*, 8 January 1993, 9.

[278] For those researchers starting out in story-based research, a useful resource is the paper on narrative inquiry by D. J. Clandinin and F. M. Connelly, 'Personal Experience Methods', in Denzin, N. and Lincoln, Y. (eds), *Handbook of Qualitative Research*, (Thousand Oaks: Sage, 1994).

[279] The following are fine examples of the five narrative types, from autobiographies to life-histories respectively: N. Hunt, *The World of Nigel Hunt*, (Beaconsfield: Darwen Finlayson, 1967); J. Deacon, *Tongue Tied*, (London: Mencap, 1974); R. Bogdan and S. Taylor, 'The Judged not the Judges', *American Psychologist*, 31, (1976), 47-52; M. V. Angrosino, 'On the Bus with Vonnie Lee', *Journal of Contemporary Ethnography*, 23, (April 1994), 14-28; and L. L. Langness and H. G. Levine (eds.), *Culture and Retardation*, (Kluwer: D. Reidel Publishing Company, 1986).

[280] This definition of *life story* and its difference to the *life history* is borrowed from I. F. Goodson 'Studying Teachers' Lives: An Emergent field of inquiry', in Goodson, I. F. (ed.), *Studying Teachers' Lives*, (New York: Teachers' College Press, 1992). For a superbly written overview of life-story research, see Ken Plummer's Documents of Life: *An Introduction to the Problems and Literature of a Humanistic Method*, (London, George Allen and Unwin, 1983).

[281] R. Whittemore, L. L. Langness and P. Koegel, 'The Life History Approach to Mental Retardation', in Langness, L. L. and Levine, H. G. (eds), *Culture and Retardation*, (Kluwer: D. Reidel Publishing Company, 1986).

[282] I. Bertaux-Wiame suggests that a story allows the reader to listen beyond the words of the storyteller and to tap into the worlds that they inhabit: 'The Life History Approach to the Study of Internal Migration', in Bertaux, D. (ed.), *Biography and Society: the Life History Approach in the Social Sciences*, (Beverly Hills: Sage, 1981).

[283] This is a commonly held view according to D. Atkinson and F. Williams, *'Know me as I am': An Anthology of Prose, Poetry and Art by People with Learning Difficulties*, (Buckingham: The Open University, 1994).

284 Bogdan and Taylor, 'The Judged not the Judges'.

285 For a very useful discussion about explaining research see J. Walmsley, 'Explaining', in Shakespeare, P., Atkinson, D. and French, S. (eds.), *Reflecting on Research Practice: Issues in Health and Social Welfare,* (Buckingham: The Open University Press, 1993).

286 T. Parker, *The Unknown Citizen,* (London: Hutchinson, 1963).

287 M. Turner, 'Literature and Social Work: An Exploration of How Literature Informs Social Work in a way Social Sciences Cannot', *British Journal of Social Work,* 21, (1991), 229-243 and J. Bruner, 'Life as Narrative', Social Research, 54, (Spring 1987), 11-32.

288 B. Harrison and E. Stina-Lyon, 'A Note on Ethical Issues in the Use of Autobiography in Sociological Research', *Sociology*, 27(1), (1993), 101-109.

289 C. B. Klockars, 'Field Ethics for the Life History', in Weppner, R. S. (ed.), *Street Ethnography,* (Beverly Hills: Sage, 1977) and S. J. Taylor and R. Bogdan, *Introduction to Qualitative Research Methods: The Search for Meanings (2nd edn.),* (New York: John Wiley and Sons, 1984).

290 J. Moffet and K. R. McElheny, *Points of View: An Anthology of Short Stories,* (New York: Signet, 1966).

291 As Tomlinson puts it, we risk ignoring the cut and thrust of contemporary political narrative and the unseen pressures of economic and structural change: S. Tomlinson, 'The Radical Structuralist View of Special Education and Disability: Unpopular Perspectives on Their Origins and Development', in Skrtic, T. M. (ed.), *Disability & Democracy: Reconstructing (Special) Education for Postmodernity,* (New York: Teachers' College Press, 1995).

292 W. F. Whyte, *Street Corner Society*, (Chicago: University of Chicago Press, 1943); W. Stott, *Documentary Expression and Thirties America,* (New York: Oxford University Press, 1973).

293 Furthermore, if, as Plummer states, the narrative researcher fails to acquire the 'necessary' skills and creative heart of the novelist, poet and artist, writing stories is further problematised - see Plummer, *Documents of Life*. According to Chatman, a weakness of the life-story method is that the narrative's plot and fable may be lacking - the product of storyteller, writer or both - see S. Chatman, 'Story and Narrative', in Walder, D. (ed.), *Literature in the Modern World,* (Oxford: Oxford University Press, 1993).

294 P. Reason and P. Hawkins, 'Storytelling as Inquiry', in Reason, P. (ed.), *Human Inquiry in Action: Developments in New Paradigm Research,* (London: Sage, 1988), p.100.

295 Audio-tapes and notes of interviews were transcribed, written up as stories, and first drafts sent to storytellers. All five changed the first drafts, a number of times in some cases, until eventually accepting the finished life-stories.

296 J. Lofland, *Analyzing Social Situations: a Guide to Qualitative Observation and Analysis,* (Belmont, California: Wardsworth, 1971); M. Tremblay, 'The Key Informant Technique: a Non-ethnographic Application', *American Anthropologist,* 59, (1959), 688-698.

297 Taylor and Bogdan, *Introduction to Qualitative Research Methods,* p.77 and pp.94-96.

[298] K. Lowe and S. de Paiva, 'Canvassing the Views of People with a Mental Handicap', *The Irish Journal of Psychology,* 9(2), (1988), 220-234; D. Atkinson, 'Research Interviews with People with Mental Handicaps', Mental Handicap Research, 1(1), (1989) 75-90; D. Atkinson, 'Relating', in Shakespeare, Atkinson and French (eds), *Reflecting on Research Practice;* B. O'Donnell, 'Resident Rights Interview', *Mental Retardation,* 14 (6), (1976),13-17; M. C. Flynn, 'Adults who are Mentally Handicapped as Consumers: Issues and Guidelines for Interviewing', *Journal of Mental Deficiency Research,* 30, (1986), 369-377; M. C. Flynn, and J. K. Saleem, 'Adults who are Mentally Handicapped and Living with their Parents: Satisfaction and Perceptions Regarding their Lives and Circumstances', *Journal of Mental Deficiency,* 30, (1986), 379-387.

[299] P. Shakespeare, 'Performing', in Shakespeare, Atkinson, and French (eds), *Reflecting on Research Practice.*

[300] R. Lawthom, 'What Can I Do? A Feminist Researcher in Non-Feminist Research', *Feminism and Psychology,* 7(4), (1997), 529-533.

[301] Taylor and Bogdan, *Introduction to Qualitative Research Methods,* pp.86.

[302] See research on 'acquiescence' by Sigelman and colleagues: including, C. Sigelman, E. Budd, C. Spanhel, and C. Schoenrock, 'When in Doubt, Say Yes: Acquiescence in Interviews with Mentally Retarded Persons', *Mental Retardation,* 19, (April, 1981) 53-58; C. Sigelman, E. Budd, J. Winer, C. Schoenrock, and P. Martin, 'Evaluating Alternative Techniques of Questioning Mentally Retarded Persons', *American Journal of Mental Deficiency,* 86(5), (1982), 511-518; C. Sigelman, C. Schoenrock, C. Spanhel, S. Hromas, J. Winer, E. Budd, P. Martin, 'Surveying Mentally Retarded Persons: Responsiveness and Response Validity in Three Samples', *American Journal of Mental Deficiency,* 84 (5), (1980), 479-486. Also for general points see M. T. Orne, 'The Nature of Hypnosis: artefact and essence', *Journal of Abnormal & Social Psychology*, 58, (1962), 277-299.

[303] See K. Simons, 'Enabling Research: People with Learning Difficulties', *Research, Policy and Planning,* 12(2), (1994), 4-5 and T. Booth and W. Booth, *Parenting under Pressure: Mothers and fathers with Learning Difficulties,* (Buckingham: Open University Press, 1994).

[304] For a readable critique of acquiescence see M. Rapley and C. Antaki (1996) A conversation analysis of the 'acquiescence' of people with learning disabilities. *Journal of Community and Applied Social Psychology,* 6, 1996, 207-227.

[305] A. Oakley, 'Interviewing Women: A Contradiction in Terms', in Roberts, H. (ed.), *Doing Feminist Research,* (London: Routledge, 1981), p.58.

[306] Tremblay, 'The Key Informant Technique'.

[307] See Plummer, *Documents of Life;* Taylor and Bogdan, *Introduction to Qualitative Research Methods,* p.91; P. March, 'Do Photographs Help Adults with Severe Mental Handicaps to Make Choices?' *British Journal of Mental Subnormality,* 28, (1992), 122-128; J. Minkes, C. Robinson and C. Weston, 'Consulting the Children: Interviews with Children using Residential Care Services', *Disability & Society,* 9(1), (1994), 47-57; J. Swain, 'Constructing Participatory Research: In Principle and in Practice', in Clough, P. and Barton, L. (eds), *Making Difficulties: Research and the Construction of SEN,* (London: Paul Chapman Ltd., 1995), p.86.

[308] S. Humphreys, G. Evans and S. Todd, *Lifelines: An Account of the Life Experiences of Seven People with a Mental Handicap who used the NIMROD Service,* (London: King Edward's Hospital Fund, 1987), p.8.

[309] C. Corradi, 'Text, Context and Individual meaning: Rethinking Life Stories in a Hermeneutic Framework', *Discourse & Society,* 2(1), (1991), 105-118.

[310] See Bertaux-Wiame, 'The Life History Approach'.

[311] Article with Bonnie Shoultz, *Thoughts about Self-advocacy,* from Internet Homepage of The Center on Human Policy, Syracuse University, New York, 1997, p.1, (http://soeweb.syr.edu/).

[312] That is, according to Angrosino, when they 'constitute a broad, heterogeneous group rather than a defined, bounded category of people, fixed within the parameters of statistical norms', (Angrosino, 'On the Bus with Vonnie Lee', p.27).

[313] 'In the course of the critical review of the interface between life events and their personal interpretation, the researcher comes to understand the individual in a way that the individual him or herself probably cannot', cited in Whittemore, Langness and Koegel, 'The Life History Approach to Mental Retardation', p.7.

[314] Reason and Hawkins, 'Storytelling as Inquiry', p.86.

[315] See Goodson, 'Studying Teachers' Lives', pp.1-7. Also, as Sparkes notes, analysis attempts to throw into sharp relief a range of structural constraints that shape storytellers' lives. See A. C. Sparkes, 'Life Histories and the Issue of Voice: Reflections on an emerging relationship', *Qualitative Studies in Education,* 7(2), (1995), 165-183.

[316] This highlights broader socio-structural, cultural, political and theoretical points, according to Whittemore, Langness and Koegel, 'The Life History Approach to Mental Retardation', p.7.

[317] H. G. Levine and L. L. Langness, 'Conclusions: Themes in an Anthropology of Mild Mental Retardation', in Langness and Levine (eds), *Culture and Retardation,* pp.192-205.

[318] L. H. Kidder and M. Fine, 'Qualitative Inquiry in Psychology: A Radical Approach', in Fox, D. and Prilleltensky, I. (eds), Critical Psychology: *An Introduction,* (London: Sage, 1997).

[319] 'The problem of analysis is hence the extent to which the researcher progressively imposes his or her 'theory' upon the understandings of the participant', cited in K. Plummer, 'Life Story Research', in Smith, J. A., Harré, R. and Langenhove, L.V. (eds), *Rethinking Methods in Psychology* (London: Sage, 1995), p.61.

[320] See C. Shaw, *The Natural History of a Delinquent Career,* (Chicago: University of Chicago Press, 1931); W. I. Thomas and F. Znaniecki, *The Polish Peasant in Europe and America, 5 vols.,* (Chicago; University of Chicago Press, 1918-1920); P. Freire, *Pedagogy of the Oppressed,* (London: Penguin, 1970).

[321] S. Aspis, *Inclusion and Exclusion,* paper presented at the Social History of Learning Disability Conference 'Inclusion and Exclusion', The Open University, Walton Hall, Milton Keynes, 10th December, 1997.

[322] See M. Humphreys, L. Hill and S. Valentine, 'A Psychotherapy Group for Young Adults with Mental Handicaps: Problems Encountered', *Mental Handicap,* 18, (September, 1990), 125-127; Turner, 'Literature and Social Work', 229-243.

[323] G. W. Allport, *The Use of Personal Documents in Psychological Science,* (New York: Social Science Research Council, 1947).

[324] 'The best stories are those which stir people's minds, hearts, souls and by doing so gives them new insights into themselves, their problems and their human condition. The challenge is to develop a human science that more fully serves this aim. The question then is not, "is story-telling science?" but "can science learn to tell good stories?"' cited in I. Mitroff and R. Kilman, *Methodological Approaches to Social Science,* (San Francisco: Jossey-Bass, 1978), p.83.

[325] This is taken further in D. Goodley, *The Politics of Resilience: Self-advocacy in the Lives of People with Learning Difficulties,* for the *Disability, Human Rights and Society* series, (Buckingham, Open University Press, forthcoming).

[326] See A. Whittaker, S. Gardener, and J. Kershaw, *Service Evaluation by People with Learning Difficulties: Based on the People First Report,* (London: King's Fund Centre, 1991); A. Whittaker, J. Kershaw and J. Spargo, 'Service Evaluation by People with Learning Difficulties', in Beresford, P. and Harding, T. (eds), *A Challenge to Change: Practical Experiences of Building User-Led Services,* (London: National Institute for Social Work, 1993); S. Aspis (see note 321 and Chapter 1 of this book); D. Atkinson, M. Jackson and J. Walmsley, *Forgotten Lives: Exploring the History of Learning Disability,* (Kidderminster: BILD, 1997); P. Mitchell, 'The Impact of Self-advocacy on Families', *Disability and Society,* 12 (1), (1997), 43-56; M. Stuart, *Different Voices, Different Communities: Stories of the Closure of a Long Stay Convent Home for Women with Learning Difficulties,* paper presented at the Social History of Learning Disability Conference, 'Inclusion and Exclusion', 10th December, 1997. See also Chapter 11 in this book.

Bibliography

Abbott, P. and Sapsford, R. (1988) 'The Body Politic, Health, Family and Society', Unit 11 of a second level Open University course, *Social Problems and Social Welfare,* Milton Keynes: The Open University Press.

Adams, M. (1995) *Those Lost Years,* Brighton: QueenSpark, Market Books.

Allport, G. W. (1947) *The Use of Personal Documents in Psychological Science,* New York: Social Science Research Council.

Anderson, J. (1990) 'The United Kingdom: Legacies of the Past', in J. Anderson and M. Ricci, (eds), *Society and Social Science: A Reader,* Milton Keynes: The Open University Press.

Andrews, J. et al. (2000) 'Scrub, Scrub, Scrub ... Bad Times and Good Times: Some of the Jobs I've done in My Life', in Atkinson, D., McCarthy, M., Walmsley, J. (eds), *Good Times: Bad Times. Stories by Women with Learning Difficulties,* Kidderminster: BILD Publications.

Angrosino, M. V. (1994) 'On the Bus with Vonnie Lee: Explorations in Life History and Metaphor', *Journal of Contemporary Ethnography,* 23 (April), 14-28.

Atkinson, D. (1988) 'Research Interviews with People with Mental Handicaps', *Mental Handicap Research,* 1(1), 75-90.

Atkinson, D. (1997) *An Auto/Biographical Approach to Learning Disability Research,* Aldershot: Ashgate.

Atkinson, D. and Williams, F. (1990) *Know me as I am: An Anthology of Prose Poetry and Art by People with Learning Difficulties,* Sevenoaks: Hodder and Stoughton.

Atkinson, D., Jackson, M. and Walmsley, J. (eds) (1997) *Forgotten Lives: Exploring the History of Learning Disability,* Kidderminster: BILD Publications.

Barker, D. (1983) 'How to Curb the Fertility of the Unfit: The Feeble Minded in Edwardian Britain', *Oxford Review of Education,* 9(3), 197-211.

Barron, D. (1996) *A Price to Be Born,* Mencap, Northern Division.

Benjacar, E. (1940) 'A mental deficiency institution in war time', *Mental Health,* 1, 107-112.

Bertaux, D. (ed.), *Biography and Society: the Life History Approach in the Social Sciences,* Beverly Hills: Sage.

Beveridge, W. (1907) 'The problem of the unemployed'. Report of a conference held by the Sociological Society, April 4, 1906, *Sociological Papers,* iii.

Bhabha, H. (1994) *The Location of Culture,* London: Routledge.

Board of Control (1936) *Suggestions and Instructions Relating To The Arrangement And Construction Of Colonies For Defectives,* London, Board of Control.

Bogdan, R., and Taylor, S. (1976) 'The Judged not the Judges: an Insider's View of Mental Retardation', *American Psychologist,* 31, 47-52.

Booth, T., and Booth, W. (1994) *Parenting under Pressure: Mothers and Fathers with Learning Difficulties,* Buckingham: Open University Press.

Bowker, G. (1993) 'The Age of Biography is upon us', *Times Higher Education Supplement,* 8 January, 9.

Brown, H. and Smith, H. (eds) (1992) *Normalisation: A Reader for the Nineties,* London: Routledge.

Brown, J. and Walton, I. (1984) *How Nurses Learn: A National Study of the Training of Nurses in Mental Handicap*, University of York.

Bruner, J. (1987) 'Life as Narrative', *Social Research,* 54 (Spring), 11-32.

Butterfield, E. C. (1961) 'A provocative case of overachievement in a mongol', *American Journal of Mental Deficiency,* 66, 444-8.

Chatman, S. (1993) 'Story and Narrative', in D. Walder (ed.), *Literature in the Modern World,* Oxford: Oxford University Press.

Chouinard, V. and Grant, A. (1996) 'Ways of Putting Ourselves in the Picture', in N. Duncan (ed.) (1996) *Body Space: Destabilising Geographies of Gender and Sexuality,* London: Routledge.

Clandinin, D. J. and Connelly, F. M. (1994) 'Personal Experience Methods', in N. Denzin and Y. Lincoln (eds), *Handbook of Qualitative Research,* Thousand Oaks, CA: Sage.

Cooper, M. (2000) 'My Quest to Find Out', in D. Atkinson, M. McCarthy, J. Walmsley, M. Cooper, S. Rolph, P. Barette, M. Coventry and G. Ferris, *Good Times, Bad Times: Women with Learning Difficulties Telling their Stories,* Kidderminster: BILD Publications.

Corradi, C. (1991) 'Text, Context and Individual Meaning: Rethinking Life Stories in a Hermeneutic Framework', *Discourse & Society,* 2(1), 105-118.

Crowther, M. A. (1981) *The Workhouse System 1834-1929: The History of an English Institution,* London: Batsford Academic and Educational Ltd.

Darwin, C. (1872) *The Origin of Species (Sixth Edition),* London: John Murray.

Darwin, R. (1926) 'The Proper Control of Defectives Outside Institutions', paper given at the 1926 Conference on Mental Welfare, Taunton.

Deacon, J. (1974) *Tongue Tied,* London: Mencap.

Delamont, S. and Duffin, L. (1978) *The Nineteenth-Century Woman: The Cultural and Physical World,* London: Croom Helm Ltd; New York: Barnes and Noble Books.

Dingwall, R., Rafferty, A. M. and Webster, C. (1998) *An Introduction to the Social History of Nursing,* London: Routledge.

Douglas, M. (1966) *Purity and Danger: An analysis of the concepts of pollution and taboo,* London and New York: Routledge.

Dowson, S. (1997) 'Empowerment within Services: A Comfortable Delusion', in Ramcharan, P., Roberts, G., Grant, G. and Borland, J. (eds) (1997) *Empowerment in Everyday Life: Learning Disability,* London: Jessica Kingsley.

Earl, J. (1997) *Dr Langdon-Down and the Normansfield Theatre,* Borough of Twickenham Local History Society.

Editorial (1865) 'Idiot Asylums', in *Edinburgh Review,* 122 (249), 37-74.

Editorial (1867) *British Medical Journal,* 22 June.

Ehrenreich, B. and English, D. (1979) *For Her Own Good: 150 Years of the Experts' Advice to Women,* London: Pluto Press.

Finlayson, G. (1990) 'A Moving Frontier: Voluntarism and the State in British Social Welfare 1911-1949', *Twentieth Century British History,* 1, 183-206.

Flynn, M. C. (1986) 'Adults who are Mentally Handicapped as Consumers: Issues and Guidelines for Interviewing', *Journal of Mental Deficiency Research,* 30, 369-377.

Flynn, M. C. and Saleem, J. K. (1986) 'Adults who are Mentally Handicapped and Living with their Parents: Satisfaction and Perceptions Regarding their Lives and Circumstances', *Journal of Mental Deficiency,* 30, 379-387.

Fortenbaugh, W. W. (1977) 'Aristotle on Slaves and Women', in J. Barnes, M. Schofield and R. Sorabji (eds), *Articles on Aristotle,* London: Duckworth, 135-139.

Fox, E. (1923) 'The Mentally Defective and the Community', *Studies in Mental Inefficiency,* 4(4), London: Central Association for Mental Welfare, 71-79.

Fox, E. (1930) 'Community Schemes for the Social Control of Mental Defectives', *Mental Welfare,* 11(3), 61-74.

Freeden, M. (1978) *The New Liberalism,* Oxford: Clarendon.

Freeman, M. D. A. (1988) 'Sterilising the Mentally Handicapped', in M. D. A. Freeman (ed.), *Medicine, Ethics and the Law,* London: Stevens and Sons.

Freire, P. (1970) *Pedagogy of the Oppressed,* London: Penguin.

Galton, F. (1883) *Inquiries into Human Faculty,* London: Macmillan and Co.

Goodley, D. (1996) 'Tales of Hidden Lives: A Critical Examination of Life History Research with People who have Learning Difficulties', *Disability & Society,* 11(3), 333-348.

Goodley, D. (1998) 'Supporting People with Learning Difficulties in Self-advocacy Groups and Models of Disability', *Health and Social Care in the Community*, 6(5), 438-446
Goodley, D. (forthcoming) 'The Politics of Resilience: Self-advocacy in the Lives of People with Learning Difficulties', for L. Barton (ed.) *Disability, Human Rights and Society* series, Buckingham: Open University Press.

Goodson, I. F. (1992) 'Studying Teachers' Lives: An Emergent field of inquiry', in I. F. Goodson (ed.), *Studying Teachers' Lives,* New York: Teachers College Press.

Greenleaf, W. H. (1983) *The British Political Tradition (Volume 1)*, London: Methuen.

Harrison, B. and Stina Lyon, E. (1993) 'A Note on Ethical Issues in the Use of Autobiography in Sociological Research', *Sociology,* 27(1), 101-109.

Hughes, B. (1999) 'The Constitution of Impairment: Modernity and the aesthetics of oppression', *Disability and Society,* 14 (2), 155-172.

Humphreys, M., Hill, L. and Valentine, S. (1990) 'A Psychotherapy Group for Young Adults with Mental Handicaps: Problems Encountered', *Mental Handicap,* 18 (September), 125-127.

Humphreys, S., Evans, G. and Todd, S. (1987) *Lifelines: An Account of the Life Experiences of Seven People with a Mental Handicap who used the NIMROD Service,* London: King Edward's Hospital Fund.

Humphries, S. (1988) *A Secret World Of Sex,* London: Sidgwick and Jackson.

Hunt, N. (1967) *The World of Nigel Hunt,* Beaconsfield: Darwen Finlayson.

International League of Societies for Persons with Mental Handicap (1994) *Just Technology?* North York: Roeher Institute.

Ireland, W. (1877) *Idiocy and Imbecility,* London: J. and A. Churchill.

Jackson, M. (1996) 'Institutional Provision for the Feeble Minded in Edwardian England', in D.Wright and A. Digby (eds), *From Idiocy to Mental Deficiency: Historical Perspectives on People with Learning Disabilities,* London: Routledge.

Jones, G. (1986) *Social Hygiene in Twentieth Century Britain,* London: Croom Helm.

Jones, K. (1972) *A History of the Mental Health Services,* London and Boston: Routledge and Kegan Paul.

Kanner, L. (1964) *A History of the Care and Study of the Mentally Retarded,* USA: Charles Thomas.

Keays-Bryne, S. (1997) 'People With Intellectual Disability and the Criminal Justice System', *Interaction,* 10 (3).

Kennedy, M. (1997) *Thoughts about Self-advocacy.* Article with Bonnie Shoultz, from Internet Homepage of The Centre on Human Policy, Syracuse University, New York (http://soeweb.syr.edu/).

Kerr, J. (1926) *The Fundamentals of School Health,* London: George Allen and Unwin Ltd.

Kidder, L. H. and Fine, M. (1997) Qualitative Inquiry in Psychology: A Radical Approach, in D. Fox and I. Prilleltensky (eds), *Critical Psychology: An Introduction,* London: Sage.

King's Fund (1988) *Ties and Connections: An Ordinary Community Life for People with Learning Difficulties,* London: King's Fund Centre.

Kitchen, R. (1998) '"Out of Place", "Knowing One's Place": space, power and the exclusion of disabled people', *Disability and Society,* 13 (3), 343-356.

Klockars, C. B. (1977) 'Field Ethics for the Life History', in R. S. Weppner (ed.), *Street Ethnography,* Beverly Hills: Sage.

Korman, N. and Glennerster, H. (1990) *Hospital Closures,* Milton Keynes: Open University Press.

Langdon-Down, J. (1866) 'Ethnic Classification of Idiots', *Clinical Lecture Reports,* London Hospital, 3.

Langness, L. L. and Levine, H. G. (eds) (1986) *Culture and Retardation,* Kluwer: D. Reidel Publishing Company.

Lawthom, R. (1997) 'What Can I Do? A Feminist Researcher in Non-Feminist Research', *Feminism and Psychology,* 7(4), 529-533.

Lewis, J. (1994) 'Gender, the family and women's agency in the building of welfare states: the British case', *Social History,* 19(1), 37-56.

Lewis, J. (1995) *The Voluntary Sector, the State and Social Work in Britain,* Aldershot: Edward Elgar.

Locke, J. [1690] (1924) *Two Treatises of Government,* London: J. M. Dent

Lofland, J. (1971) *Analyzing Social Situations: a Guide to Qualitative Observation and Analysis,* Belmont, California: Wardsworth.

Lowe, K. and De Paiva, S. (1988) 'Canvassing the Views of People with a Mental Handicap', *The Irish Journal of Psychology,* 9(2), 220-234.

March, J., Steingold, B., Justice, S. and Mitchell, P. (1997) 'Follow the Yellow Brick Road! People with Learning Difficulties as Co-researchers', *British Journal of Learning Disabilities,* 25, 77-80.

March, P. (1992) 'Do Photographs Help Adults with Severe Mental Handicaps to Make Choices?' *British Journal of Mental Subnormality,* 28, 122-128.

Miles, R. (1989) 'Representations of the Other', in *Racism,* London: Routledge, Chapman and Hall.

Minkes, J., Robinson, C. and Weston, C. (1994) 'Consulting the Children: Interviews with Children using Residential Care Services', *Disability and Society,* 9(1), 47-57.

Mitchell, D. (1996) 'Learning disability nursing in the post war period', *International History of Nursing Journal*, 1, 20-33.

Mitchell, D. (1998) 'Learning disability nursing: reflections on history', *Journal of Learning Disabilities for Nursing, Health and Social Care,* 2, 45-49.

Mitchell, P. (1997) 'The Impact of Self-advocacy on Families', *Disability and Society,* 12(1), 43-56.

Mitchell, P. (1998) *Self-advocacy and Families,* Unpublished PhD thesis: Open University.

Mitroff, I. and Kilman, R. (1978) *Methodological Approaches to Social Science,* San Francisco: Jossey-Bass.

Moffett, J. and McElheny, K. R. (1966) *Points of View: An Anthology of Short Stories,* New York: Signet.

National Council For Civil Liberties (1951) '50,000 Outside the Law: An examination of the treatment of those certified as mentally defective', London: NCCL.

Nightingale, F. (1859) *Notes on Nursing: what is it and what it is not*, Edinburgh: Churchill Livingstone.

Nolan, P. (1993) *A History of Mental Health Nursing*, London: Chapman and Hall.

Oakley, A. (1976) *Housewife,* Harmondsworth: Penguin Books.

Oakley, A. (1981) 'Interviewing Women: A Contradiction in Terms', in H. Roberts (ed.), *Doing Feminist Research,* London: Routledge.

O'Donnell, B. (1976) 'Resident Rights Interview', *Mental Retardation,* 14(6), 13-17.

Oliver, M. (1990) *The Politics of Disablement,* Houndmills, Basingstoke, Hampshire, London: The Macmillan Press Ltd.

Open University (1996) *Learning Disability: Working as Equal People,* Milton Keynes: Open University Press.

Opie, A. (1992) 'Qualitative Research Appropriation of the "Other" and Empowerment', *Feminist Review,* 40, Spring 1992, 52-70.

Orne, M. T. (1962) 'The Nature of Hypnosis: artefact and essence', *Journal of Abnormal and Social Psychology,* 58, 277-299.

Oswin, M. (1971) *The Empty Hours,* London, Allen Lane: The Penguin Press.

Oswin, M. (1978) *Children Living in Long-Stay Hospitals,* London: Heinemann Medical, Spastics International Medical Publications Research Monograph No.5.

Parker, T. (1963) *The Unknown Citizen,* London: Hutchinson.

Penton, J. (1992) 'Meeting special needs. Waverley School, Enfield, and the Red Cross Centre, Irvine', *Architects' Journal,* 9 September.

Philo, C. (1987) '"Fit localities for an asylum": the historical geography of the "mad-business" in England viewed through the pages of the Asylum Journal', *Journal of Historical Geography,* 13, 398-415.

Plummer, K. (1983) *Documents of Life: An Introduction to the Problems and Literature of a Humanistic Method,* London: George Allen and Unwin.

Plummer, K. (1995) 'Life Story Research', in J. A. Smith, R. Harré, and L. V. Langenhove (eds), *Rethinking Methods in Psychology,* London: Sage.

Poovey, M. (1988) *Uneven Developments: The Ideological Work of Gender in Mid-Victorian England,* London: Virago.

Potts, M. and Fido, R. (1991) *'A Fit Person to be Removed': Personal Accounts of Life in a Mental Deficiency Institution,* Plymouth: Northcote House.

Potts, P. (1982) 'Origins', Unit 9 of Open University course, *Special Needs in Education,* Milton Keynes: Open University Press.

Potts, P. (1983) 'Medicine, Morals and Mental Deficiency', in *Oxford Review of Education,* 9(3), 81-196.

Pufendorf, S. (1717) *Of the Laws of Nature and Nations* (Third Edition), Basil Kennet translator with the notes of Jean Barbeyrac, London.

Rafferty, A. M. (1996) *The Politics of Nursing Knowledge,* London: Routledge.

Ramcharan, P., Roberts, G., Grant, G. and Borland, J. (1997) Citizenship, Empowerment and Everyday Life: Ideal and Illusion in the New Millennium, in P. Ramcharan, G. Roberts, G. Grant and J. Borland (eds) *Empowerment in Everyday Life: Learning Disability,* London: Jessica Kingsley.

Reason, P. and Hawkins, P. (1988) 'Storytelling as Inquiry', in P. Reason (ed.), *Human Inquiry in Action: Developments in New Paradigm Research,* London: Sage.

Richardson, K. (ed.) (1972) *Race, Culture and Intelligence,* Harmondsworth: Penguin.

Ringshall, R., Miles, M. and Kelsall, F. (1983) *The Urban School. Buildings for Education in London 1870-1980,* London: Greater London Council and The Architectural Press.

Rosen, M., Clark, G. R, and Kivitz, M. S. (1976) *The History of Mental Retardation, Collected Papers, Volume 1,* Baltimore: University Park Press.

Ryan, J. and Thomas, R. (1980) *The Politics of Mental Handicap,* Harmondsworth, Middlesex, England; New York: Penguin Books.

Scull, A. (1977) *Decarceration,* USA, Princeton: Prentice-Hall.

Searle, R. (1976) *Eugenics and Politics In Britain: 1900-1914,* Leyden: Noordhoff.

Séguin, E. (1866) *Idiocy: And its Treatment by the Physiological Method,* Albany, New York: Brandow Printing Company.

Shakespeare, P. Atkinson, D. and French, S. (eds) (1993) *Reflecting on Research Practice: Issues in Health and Social Welfare,* Buckingham: Open University Press.

Shaw, C. (1931) *The Natural History of a Delinquent Career,* Chicago: University of Chicago Press.

Shennan, V. (1980) *Our Concern: The Story of the National Association for Mentally Handicapped Children and Adults,* London: National Association for Mentally Handicapped Children and Adults.

Sibley, D. (1995) *Geographies of Exclusion,* London: Routledge.

Sigelman, C. K., Budd, E. C., Winer, J. L., Schoenrock, C. J. and Martin, P. W. (1982) 'Evaluating Alternative Techniques of Questioning Mentally Retarded Persons', *American Journal of Mental Deficiency,* 86(5), 511-518.

Sigelman, C. K., Schoenrock, C. J., Spanhel, C. L., Hromas, S. G., Winer, J. L., Budd, E. C. and Martin, P. W. (1980) 'Surveying Mentally Retarded Persons: Responsiveness and Response Validity in Three Samples', *American Journal of Mental Deficiency,* 84(5), 479-486.

Sigelman, C. K., Budd, E. C., Spanhel, C. L. and Schoenrock, C. (1981) 'When in Doubt, Say Yes: Acquiescence in Interviews with Mentally Retarded Persons', *Mental Retardation,* 19, April, 53-58.

Simmons, H. (1982) *From Asylum to Welfare,* Downsview: NIMR.

Simons, K. (1994) 'Enabling Research: People with Learning Difficulties', *Research, Policy and Planning,* 12(2), 4-5.

Sorabji, R. (1993) *Animal Minds and Human Values: The Origins of the Western Debate,* Ithica: Cornell University Press.

Sparkes, A. C. (1994) 'Life Histories and the Issue of Voice: Reflections on an emerging relationship', *Qualitative Studies in Education,* 7(2), 165-183.

Stafford-Clark, D. (1950) *Psychiatry Today* (1973 edition), Harmondsworth: Penguin.

Stainton, T. (1994) *Autonomy and Social Policy,* Aldershot: Avebury.

Stainton, T. (1998) 'Intellectual Disability, Difference and Oppression', in Bogdan Lesnik (ed.), *Countering Discrimination in Social Work,* Aldershot: Ashgate/Arena.

Stainton, T. (1998) 'Rights and Rhetoric in Policy and Practice', in A. Symonds and A. Kelly (eds), *The Social Construction of Community Care,* London: Macmillan.

Stott, W. (1973) *Documentary Expression and Thirties America,* New York: Oxford University Press.

Sutcliffe, J. and Simons, K. (1993) *Self-advocacy and Adults with Learning Difficulties: Contexts and Debates,* Leicester: The National Institute of Adult Continuing Education in Association with The Open University Press.

Swain, J. (1995) 'Constructing Participatory Research: In Principle and in Practice', in P. Clough and L. Barton (eds), *Making Difficulties: Research and the Construction of SEN,* London: Paul Chapman Ltd.

Symonds, A. and Kelly, A. (eds) (1998) *The Social Construction of Community Care,* Basingstoke: Macmillan.

Taylor, S. J. and Bogdan, R. (1984) *Introduction to Qualitative Research Methods: The Search for Meanings (2nd edition),* New York: John Wiley & Sons.

Thane, P. (1996) *The Foundations of the Welfare State* (2nd edition), Harlow: Longman.

Thomas, W. I. and Znaniecki, F. (1918-20) *The Polish Peasant in Europe and America* (5 vols.), Chicago: University of Chicago Press.

Thompson, P. (1988) *The Voice of the Past: Oral History (2nd edition),* Oxford: Oxford University Press.

Thomson, M. (1996) *The 'Problem' of Mental Deficiency in England and Wales 1913 - 1946,* Oxford: Clarendon Press.

Thomson, M. (1998) *The Problem of Mental Deficiency: Eugenics, Democracy and Social Policy in Britain c.1870-1959,* Oxford: Clarendon Press.

Tomlinson, S. (1995) 'The Radical Structuralist View of Special Education and Disability: Unpopular Perspectives on Their Origins and Development', in T. M. Skrtic (ed.) *Disability & Democracy: Reconstructing (Special) Education for Postmodernity,* New York: Teachers College Press.

Tredgold, A. F. (1908) *Mental Deficiency,* London: Balliere, Tindall & Cox.

Tredgold, A. F. (1911) 'Eugenics and the Future Progress of Man', *Eugenics Review,* 3, (Apr., 1911 – Jan., 1912), 94-117.

Tremblay, M. (1959) 'The Key Informant Technique: a Non-Ethnographic Application', *American Anthropologist,* 59, 688-698.

Trent, J.W. (1994) *Inventing the Feeble Mind: A History of Mental Retardation in the United States*, University of California Press.

Turner, F. D. (1920) 'Notes about institutions for defectives', *Studies in Mental Inefficiency,* 1, 32-38.

Turner, M. (1991) 'Literature and Social Work: An Exploration of How Literature Informs Social Work in a way Social Sciences Cannot', *British Journal of Social Work,* 21, 229-243.

Walker, A. and Moulton, R. (1989) 'Photo Albums: Images of Time and Reflections of Self', *Qualitative Sociology*, 12(2), 164-165.

Walmsley, J (1993) 'Contradictions in Caring: Reciprocity and Interdependence', *Disability, Handicap and Society,* 8(2), 129-141.

Walmsley, J. (1994) *Gender, Caring and Learning Disability,* Unpublished PhD Thesis, The Open University.

Walmsley, J., Atkinson, D. and Rolph, S. (1999) 'Community Care and Mental Deficiency', in P. Bartlett and D. Wright (eds), *Outside the Walls of the Asylum,* London: Athlone.

Webb, S. and Webb, B. (eds) (1909) *The Break-Up of the Poor Law: Being Part One of The Minority Report of The Poor Law Commission*, London: Longmans, Green and Co.

Wedgwood, C.V. (1951) *The Last of the Radicals,* London: Johnathan Cape.

Wedgwood, J. C. (1940) *Memoirs of a Fighting Life,* London: Hutchinson.

Whittaker, A., Gardener, S., and Kershaw, J. (1991) *Service Evaluation by People with Learning Difficulties: Based on the People First Report,* London: King's Fund Centre.

Whittaker, A., Kershaw, J. and Spargo, J. (1993) 'Service Evaluation by People with Learning Difficulties', in P. Beresford and T. Harding (eds), *A Challenge to Change: Practical Experiences of Building User-Led Services,* London: National Institute for Social Work.

Whyte, W. F. (1943) *Street Corner Society*, Chicago: University of Chicago Press.

Williams, F. (1992) 'Women with Learning Difficulties are Women Too', in M. Langan and L. Day (eds), *Women, Oppression and Social Work: Issues in Anti-Discriminatory Practice,* London: Unwin Hyman.

Wolfensberger, W. (1972) *The Principle of Normalisation in Human Services,* Toronto: National Institute for Mental Retardation.

Wright, D. and Digby, A. (eds) (1996) *From Idiocy to Mental Deficiency: Historical Perspectives on People with Learning Disabilities,* London: Routledge.